W9-CAF-449

Be a Better Parent

Be a Better Parent

Mary Margaret Kern

Turkeyfoot Reading Center
Confluence, PA 15424

The Westminster Press
Philadelphia

Copyright © 1979 The Westminster Press

All rights reserved—no part of this book may be reproduced in any form without permission in writing from the publisher, except by a reviewer who wishes to quote brief passages in connection with a review in magazine or newspaper.

Scripture quotations from the Revised Standard Version of the Bible are copyrighted 1946, 1952, © 1971, 1973 by the Division of Christian Education of the National Council of the Churches of Christ in the U.S.A., and are used by permission.

First edition

Published by The Westminster Press ®

Philadelphia, Pennsylvania

PRINTED IN THE UNITED STATES OF AMERICA

9 8 7 6 5 4 3 2 1

Library of Congress Cataloging in Publication Data

Kern, Mary Margaret, 1906–
  Be a better parent.

  1. Parenting—United States. 2. Social values.
3. Socialization. 4. Family—Religious life.
I. Title.
HQ755.8.K47   261.8'34'27   79–9098
ISBN 0–664–24271–5

For My Family
Herb
Flora Jane, Bruce, Sara

Contents

Acknowledgments

Much of the material in this book appeared originally as articles in *Discovery* and *Opening Doors,* published by the Board of Christian Education of The United Presbyterian Church in the U.S.A.

The following topics appeared in *Home Life,* published by the Sunday School Board of the Southern Baptist Convention: "Watch Them Grow," "That Positive Approach," "Church Away from Home," "Your Child and Death," "When We Worship at Home," "Confidences Must Be Earned," and "The Masks We Wear." These additional themes appeared in *The Christian Home,* published by The Graded Press of The United Methodist Church: "Health Habits Are Wealth Habits," "Is Politeness Out of Date?" "Does It Really Matter?" and "No More Idle Threats."

"Why Not Hymns at Home?" is based on an article that appeared in *Mother's Magazine,* David C. Cook Publishing Company.

Introduction

The hand of the parent writes on the
heart of the child the first faint characters
which time deepens into strength so that
nothing can efface them.

Rowland Hill

Being a parent is a learning experience. It can be said, "Parents are made, not born." While the instincts for parenting are there, given by God, they must be brought out into the open, refined and put to use by each of us depending on the individual situation.

The early years of a child are the important time, whether or not we believe the adage that the first seven years determine all that follows. In a more practical sense the early years, perhaps through the sixth grade in school, are the years when children are at home *with* parents, when they are dependent *on* parents, when (at times) they listen *to* parents. After that, at least partially, we lose them.

Much of the material in this book is a firsthand recounting of our family happenings with our three children during their early years, not necessarily appearing in time sequence. Also included are other, more general stories, still coming out of personal, contemporary experiences from the life-style of additional families.

The book does not pretend to be the be-all and know-all of parenthood. Rather, it hopes to give parents the courage to be themselves as parents and to share philosophies and ideals which parents can impart to children that, with God's help, will "deepen into strength so that nothing can efface them."

I

As Parents– We Build Attitudes

Whatever you would have your children become, strive to exhibit in your own lives and conversation.

Lydia H. Sigourney

No One Can Win
All the Time

A good loser has a head start on learning to accept life, its good and bad included

The two second-graders had the game spread out on our living room floor. When I came to remind them that Gracie had better go home since it was almost time to eat, my own Sara lifted her head quickly. "She can't go home. She's ahead. She has to stay until I catch up!"

The desire to win possesses all of us. Sara, who is our family game-hound, started wanting to win when, at about four years of age, she and I first held a few simple cards in hand and tried to match the animal pictures with the animal noises that we tried to imitate. It was hilarious—but under the laughter, Sara could scarcely bear to lose the game to me. Later, when we had progressed to parcheesi, I found myself considering the difference in our ages and abilities and sometimes holding myself in check in order to give her a chance to win.

On the other hand, learning to lose is tremendously important. Children make short shrift of the poor loser. I overheard a group of children once unmercifully taunting another child. "Stop being a spoilsport!" they said. "No one wants to play with you if you act like *that* when you're behind."

How can we help a child learn to be a good loser? An early, and quite important, opportunity for this comes when a child is first in school, plays games outside the family circle, and meets up with competition in other areas where, as likely as not, he may be defeated.

In our case, the first stiff realization of what it means to be a loser came to Sara when she traded me as a game partner and took on her older sister. I noticed at once that there was no sentimental leeway in this relationship. Older sister won most of the games now. Sara was at first wont to bemoan it, then she grew a little angry, and from this she doggedly went on, still playing and still trying to win. Fortunately, older sister supplied the ingredient that would help Sara learn to be a good loser. She constantly tempered her winning with the words: "But it's only a game. When you play a game, someone has to lose. No one can win all the time."

This attitude seems to me important, especially since we adults often appear to belie it with *our* actions. What about the colleges that promptly fire the football coach of a losing team? In the eyes of some alumni, apparently, no one should lose a football game, which, considering the nature of the contest, is a little hard to bring about.

However, it's no good to expect a child not to display disappointment on losing, whether it's just in a game at home with the family, in a three-legged race at Dad's Rotary Club picnic, or dropping clothespins into a bottle at a birthday party. Of course a child is disappointed, particularly if he did his best, and he has a right to say so, providing he (1) doesn't whine, (2) doesn't make up useless excuses for himself, and (3) keeps cheerful in his outlook as to what he'll do next time. The stiff upper lip and the handshake after the tennis match, with the suitably murmured words of congratulation, come later, if at all, for even these are of no use if the feelings underneath are not right.

It is the feelings that we parents should be most concerned with. A child who learns to accept game playing as fun and no great crisis, win or lose, is fast on the way to learning how to lose well in other areas and feel right about it.

For never mistake it! Life is made up of a series of game type activities, many of them ending in losses, some of them

serious. And the odds are by no means even. Sometimes the
people you are competing with are older and smarter, or
possibly even your age or younger, but just smarter anyway.
Sometimes illness holds you back; sometimes actual bad luck
seems to take over. One way or another, you can only play
the game the best you know how. If you win, fine. If not, what
then?

Two men sought promotions in their separate companies.
Neither one was promoted. How did each respond? Well, one
could scarcely sleep, made his family miserable, and nearly
had a nervous breakdown over it. The other one, feeling his
defeat no less strongly, was quiet about it. He just went on
working. All he said was: "Of course, I'm disappointed. But
I'm still trying."

Fortunately, children cannot foresee the future and thus
realize that from simple defeats in hopscotch and parcheesi
they will go on to more serious matters. But they receive a
smattering of it nowadays in very early years. (I contend that
in the dim, uncomplicated past, we were not subjected to so
many pressures so often!)

In one school I know, there is a student council for the
little ones—an excellent idea, I suppose, but it means an
election for the representative from each room. After names
have been put up for the job, the two children who have been
nominated put their heads down on their desks while the rest
vote, by hands.

So, you are eight years old and you have already been
defeated for office! Do you whine and fret about it? Or do you
accept it and go on about your business?

Acceptance is hardly a word you would use in talking to
an eight-year-old. Yet it is, after all, the crux of this matter.
A young man was stricken with two types of infantile paraly-
sis. Though he was gravely ill, even requiring an incision in
his throat for a tube so that he might breathe, he still exuded
confidence and courage. The hospital staff finally put him,
sick as he was, in a room with less ill polio patients whose
spirits were poor, so that he might help them.

Curious and inspired, I asked his mother, "What is it about Kent that makes his attitude so outstanding?"

"I don't know exactly," she replied, "except he's always been good at accepting the things that come to him."

Thus, the child who was defeated for student council; the child who wants to make straight A's, like his sister, but doesn't; the child who tries to make the team, but can't, has to figure out how to be a good loser or, in other words, a good accepter. If in the early years he has learned that in every game or contest at least one person has to lose and no one can win all the time, then he has a head start on learning to accept life, its good and bad included.

This child also will begin, in a small way, to accept himself, his own good and bad included. Maybe he is not as outgoing and thus not as popular (and never will be) as Billy Smith, who won the student council job. Maybe he is not as gifted as his sister, who gets those straight A's; and, work as he will, he never will be. And maybe he does not have the build for playing football and cannot ever be on the team, no matter how he tries.

In all these cases, all a child can do is the best he can with the talents God gave him—and go right on, trying and trying, winning or losing, all the days of his life.

Is Money Necessary?

Who does not complain sometimes, "We just don't have enough money"?

The letter came early one Sunday, for it was the holiday season, with mailmen working overtime. Two of our children had just arisen.

Opening the Christmas cards, I couldn't avoid an involuntary "Oh!" when I came to the one from Barbara. "Listen to this!" I said. "Barbara's husband has been made a vice-president of his company. They have a swimming pool in their backyard. Here's a picture of their estate—"

The children swarmed over me, grabbing the picture.

"Their older son has a car of his own," I reported, reading on. "And Barbara has a mink coat."

The children had an awesome thought. "Do you *really* know these people, Mother?"

When I nodded, our young daughter had another thought. "I know somebody like that too. His father bought him a pony."

Our daughter's thought moved on with (to her) inexorable logic. "I'd like a pony, but you say we haven't enough money. I wish we had more money."

It wasn't solely our daughter's statement about money that concerned me. What about other children—yours as well as mine—and the children all up and down our streets in America? Is the belief growing that getting what you want in life comes from having money?

Actually, the young child's interest in money is usually so fleeting it practically isn't there. I'll never forget when this daughter, at age seven, refused the several nickels her dad offered her for her weekly allowance. "My purse is too full of nickels already," she gave as her reason.

When children grow older, however, their ideas may change. I have a high school teacher friend. He tells about a conversation with a boy in his class. "When I graduate from high school, what I want to do is make a lot of money," he announced with the fierceness of youth. "I haven't time to do that extra reading you want me to. I'm not going to bother with college. I'm going to start now getting around meeting people, making connections."

His teacher tried to tell him he didn't know half enough about life. "Happiness is the really important thing in life," my friend told him. "Money won't bring you that."

The boy only laughed. "I'll take a chance on the money."

Unfortunately, lots of us—both parents and others—don't do much better than that boy in our thinking. Most of us know that "money isn't everything," but it's hard to remember it. Advertising constantly reminds us that we should have timesaving equipment in shining modern kitchens, glossy new rugs in picture-window living rooms, color television in knotty-pine dens and game-room basements. What can bring all this to us but money?

By way of contrast, a friend of my mother's who grew up in the early twentieth century says cheerfully: "We were terribly poor, but we children never knew it. We were perfectly happy." And in other days, of course, my great-grandmother, a widow, was able to get by for a whole year on about eighty dollars in cash, supplementing this with fruits and vegetables she canned from her garden, a little produce received from country relatives, and a small sewing job.

But, let's face it, as the youngsters say. Today we live in a world where money has tremendous importance. How can we help our children meet this fact, yet guide them to understand that true happiness and success in life have nothing to do with money?

First, it seems to me that we can let a little maturity seep into our own lives and not express envy for those material goods which our neighbors have that we haven't. It's all right to show excitement when the children come racing in and say that a neighbor has a new white car, and it's all right to express wonder and awe over it. But it's not necessary to continue, when hubby comes home, with the plaint: "I wish *we* had a car like the Joneses. Our old car surely looks beat up beside theirs. Why can't *we* ever have nice new things like other people?"

Second, we can try to combat a peculiarly modern problem. When someone agrees to do a job, the response often is, "What'll you give me for it?" We seem to have lost the conviction of our forefathers that a job is worth doing for itself, that no matter how long it takes, a job must be well done (what, no overtime?). A way to de-emphasize this attitude at home is by expecting many jobs to be done "for free," simply because we are a family and we work together. Only the extras—digging dandelions, raking leaves—would be done for pay. Jobs poorly done or left incomplete ("Mom, I'm going to play now!") would not receive the full rate.

Third, we can learn to find the joys in life that money can't buy and point them out to our children: the song of the robin in an early spring dawn, the lingering glory of a sunset, baby sister's first wavering smile, the tingly feeling of well-being that comes from a swift game of tennis. These are only a few of the tangibles in life that are priceless. And there are intangibles that money can't buy, too, such as friendship and love and happiness. Even a little child begins to understand early that it's the friendship he *gives* freely to others that brings true satisfaction.

Also, we can sacrifice some things money can buy for the greater satisfaction of doing for others. It's not terribly fashionable nowadays to give up for others. What will the neighbors think if, to save money, you keep wearing the coat that's gone out of fashion, even if it is still good? But money given to the church, to the Red Cross, to the Community Fund, on down to the little gift for that lonely old lady on the street is repaid a thousand times. Children who themselves are loved readily learn to give freely. Knowing that it is truly more blessed to give than to receive, we find that the love of giving can bring joy throughout life.

I've always felt touched by the joy our young daughter felt when she took that same purse of hers "too full of nickels" and used the money to buy me a gift. It was a yellow hankie to match my yellow dress. All smiles, she confided to me that night at bedtime: "Now my purse is empty. I spent it all!" I marveled at the happiness in her voice. At that point, empty or full, her purse was not the center of her life.

Next, we can practice faith, not fear, when money is needed and not forthcoming. So much has been said about being secure that we are likely to depend on old-age pensions, social security benefits, and the like. But as worthwhile and important as these are, if we come to a moment when life strikes hard at us, we need some other resource. God is great enough to sustain us, no matter how large the trouble or difficulty. And our children need to learn from us that it's not money which gives us security—it's faith in God.

Finally, it's not hard to handle this idea that money can get you what you want in life *if* you know what you want. But do you know? How long has it been since you thought about your life's goal? If your goal is the Christian one of doing God's will—well, that puts money values in a secondary position. If we teach our children that life gains its true direction through our willingness to go where God leads, to do what he wants us to do, money will take its rightful place in our twentieth-century living. Although nowadays we can't live without it, with God's help we can live wisely with it.

This Honesty Business

We can't make a child honest; we can only lead the child toward honesty

My friend and I were talking. "I'm worried," she confided. "I found two strange toy autos among Tommy's things. I'm sure he brought them home from a place where he plays. Does that mean he's starting to steal?"

Admitting that I didn't know, I thought it sounded bad. Only now, when I have a family of my own and have had occasion to learn more about children's habits, I realize that for the normal child such a situation may not mean anything serious. Often the very young child does not clearly distinguish between "mine" and "thine." Anything he wants very much becomes his, he thinks, for the taking. Even at seven years of age he does not have a complete understanding of truthfulness and honesty. This allows him to pick up a friend's two autos, as Tommy did, without much thought. Studies show that though he's more truthful than he was at age six, he's still learning.

For me the key word in this is *learning*. We need to remember that it may take several years for a child to understand honesty and to learn from experience to be honest in various circumstances.

That's not to say that slipups in all children are uncomplicated. A little girl who helped herself to a small present that another child had brought to their Sunday church school teacher admitted she wanted the present for her mother. Those of us who knew the home situation, harassed by poverty and lack of love, sensed that this child's dishonest act was really a call for help.

But for your child and my child, and all the other children who are not insecure but just working at growing up normally, the problem is simpler, though we still need to look for hidden motives when we discover small dishonesties. Our best tools are understanding and patience, while we try to explain clearly what is the right of the matter. Perhaps we can remember some childhood mistake of our own, as does Helen. "I sneaked off with some paper dolls once," she admits. "Though I never returned them, I was bothered. I never played with them. And I can truthfully say this was the only time in my whole life I ever did anything like that."

But stealing is only one facet of the problem. What about lying? One preschooler, forbidden to play in the snow, went anyway. When confronted, he denied it, despite the fact that his feet were wet and his hands icy! And so naive was his thinking that later he happily volunteered how much fun it had been to throw snowballs.

Few people would accuse this boy of really lying. This very small child, so innocent and transparent in his falsehoods, is easily forgiven. Unfortunately, we are not so tolerant of the older child. Once he is in school, we have a notion that he should "know better." We don't always realize that this child is also groping.

Nevertheless it may be too charitable to say that two boys who resorted to a form of dishonesty when they tried to plan a marshmallow roast over an open trash fire were still groping. Racing to one of their moms to borrow long forks and a box of marshmallows, the boys solemnly assured her that, yes, they had already asked permission of the other mom who agreed that toasting was a great idea. And yes, it would be perfectly safe, since the other mom was planning to watch the fire (and them) while they toasted.

However, mothers of boys this age sometimes are suspicious. A phone call provided the information that what the boys had said was not true. The fire-building mom knew nothing of the marshmallow-toasting plan or of her role as fire warden.

In this instance, the excitement of the moment may have led the boys into lying. It also illustrates that shading the truth (and playing one parent against the other) most often occurs in situations where a child feels from past experience that the answer to a request may be no. Unfortunately, figuring ways to get around parental rules and disapproval can become almost a game for some children later in life.

Fortunately, these young boys apparently realized that their duplicity wasn't working and, instead of showing up at the fire, ran and hid for the rest of the afternoon—thus forfeiting their chance to toast marshmallows and providing their own punishment, of a sort.

The first time a child of this age stands up and admits wrongdoing is really a time for rejoicing.

Such a time finally came for one six-year-old. Though overage, she was regularly put to bed for naps. Each day her mother would ask, "Did you sleep, honey?" Knowing she was supposed to sleep and being fearful that her mother would scold her if she hadn't done so, the little girl always answered yes. But finally her conscience prodded her into admitting breathlessly: "I never sleep. I'm not sleepy. I haven't been telling the truth."

Luckily for this child, her mother had been trusting and was appreciative, too, of the confession. With our adult standards nagging us, this sort of trust and appreciation is sometimes hard to achieve; yet it is well worth cultivating.

To admit wrongdoing is difficult even for adults. I had this brought home to me when I accidentally cracked a fine antique saucer while wiping dishes for my mother-in-law. Besides feeling stupid for being so clumsy, I found it took a good bit of prodding of myself to make me show the dish to her and explain. It would have been so much simpler to put it away in the cupboard, where, when found later, its breakage would probably not have been connected with me at all!

Significantly, along with my embarrassed and contrite feelings in this situation, no fear was involved. I knew I would not be spanked, deprived of privileges, or made to pay for what I had done. Think how hard it must be for a child who, besides being uncertain about his actions, is all too often scared about what we may do to him! Is it any wonder that he may undertake to lie his way out of his dilemma?

It's possible, too, that at times we don't set a good example. Maybe your child hears you say over the phone that you can't help with the church supper because you don't feel well today, yet your child knows you never felt better! Maybe your child hears his father talk, too, about ways of getting out of paying some of his income tax.

A college professor told the members of his psychology class to keep careful account of every small dishonesty for a couple of weeks. These reasonably honest young people were surprised to find out the number of white—and not so white —lies they told or were tempted to tell during that period.

It's a delicate balance we try to achieve in this honesty business. It's important to let a child know the goal: complete honesty in word and deed, in a world whose ruler is the God of truth. Yet, if we remember that the young child is *still learning,* we can trust him more and give him more love and understanding when correcting his mistakes. We can also watch ourselves to be aware of our own inconsistencies.

Certainly along this line we should try not to make a child fearful, since some kind of fear is the cause of most childish lying. Above all, we must remember we can't *make* a child honest, we can only lead the child toward honesty. The decision—or, rather, the endless series of decisions—between falsehood and truth he must make himself.

Watch Them Grow

Giving children responsibilities develops their personality and character—it also takes a burden off parents

When our daughter Sara turned seven, just past the eager-beaver stage of the preschooler and just old enough to begin doing things on her own, her dad and I tried to lead her gradually into taking responsibility and doing more and more on her own. We were pleased to note the growth in character and experience that responsibility brought.

One of the first things Sara did alone was to go to the store for me. On the surface, this may not look like much, since she had been going to the store with me during most of her short life.

But going alone was different. As Sara couldn't read much yet, it was necessary to describe the loaf of bread I wanted by explaining the color and design on the wrapper. Then I told Sara to take her purchase to a checker we knew well, give her the money, and let her make change.

Off Sara went, clutching the money in her damp palm, her face shining with joy at the new experience before her.

Soon she returned, her face wreathed in smiles, the brown paper sack with the bread under her arm. When she dropped several coins into my hand I knew that she had learned firsthand about change.

There were other things she had to learn firsthand. The next time I sent her for bread she rushed home to tell me that the kind of bread I usually bought wasn't there. This was after I had already instructed her to buy any kind of bread if our brand was sold out. But she wanted to be doubly sure before she did.

Later I increased the shopping list and added eggs and catsup to it. The eggs she immediately selected according to the color of the carton, but the catsup was harder. She ran home that time, too, to verify the spelling of C-A-T-S-U-P on the bottle before purchasing it.

It pleased me that she was so careful. Actually, it was the first job she had ever done alone with grown-up responsibility.

Taking mail to the post office was next. That means responsibility, too, not for money, but for important letters that mustn't be lost or dropped in the mud (in a moment of absent-mindedness).

Sara was delighted with this also. But even though she had frequently been to the post office, as to the grocery, I soon discovered she didn't know much about that either. I solved this by drawing a picture of the various slots where mail is dropped and marked the one where this particular letter was to go. Off she went, holding the letter and the picture tightly, completely confident that she could do the job at hand.

Do it she did, and then graduated to buying stamps, for which, at first, I sent a note listing my needs.

At this age, the number of trips to our little village square, which was close enough to our house and safe enough as to traffic to allow this running back and forth, never mattered to her. The more trips the better! She wanted to pay the electric bill for me too. Wanted to take the phone bill around the corner to the telephone office. Wanted to have a basket put on her bike so that when she rode to town she could carry more letters, groceries, whatever.

The most obvious result of all this, of course, was that it was helpful to have Sara run errands for me. But I was actually more interested in less obvious results. Besides all she was learning through experience about everyday living, it was immediately apparent that Sara was taking pride in doing these jobs as well as Mother and Dad could do them. Since doing a job thoroughly and well is one of the important musts of life, we were understandably pleased with this attitude.

Sara's first experience in independence—handling her own business—was checking her shoe length at the shoe store. I'd been thinking for some time that she was outgrowing her dress-up shoes but hadn't gotten around to checking on it. When I mentioned it to her, she bugged me to let her go alone. At the small family shoe store where we went, Sara knew the salesman well. He always kidded her and made jokes, while being very patient with her often stubborn ideas about what she did and didn't like about the shoes he showed her. Besides, he was completely trustworthy. I knew he wouldn't try to sell me shoes we didn't need.

So I let Sara go to the store wearing her dress-up shoes and carrying a note asking how soon we should buy new ones. I watched her march off, pleased and happy. It seemed to me her back was a little straighter than usual, and I knew for a fact she felt good all through. When she returned she was running. Her face was flushed and she was triumphant.

Yes, she'd managed the one street she'd had to cross all right, even though there was a school bus parked and blocking the way. This unexpected hazard made her even happier because she'd figured out how to get around it.

Yes, Mr. Moore had measured her shoes, put a pad in the heels where they were rubbing, and sent a note back. She handed me the note, but before I read it she informed me: "I don't need shoes for a while. But about Easter time, Mr. Moore says I'll want some for the Easter parade!"

Understanding the other fellow's job is something else that's important. Some things Mothers and Dads have to do are downright hard work, and usually children have no conception of this. But when Sara jumped in to shovel snow she learned why Dad is out of breath every time he has to clear the walks after a snowstorm.

"I'm hot," Sara announced when she came in, shaking snow all over the back hall as she shrugged off her coat. And indeed she was perspiring from the shoveling.

She propelled me eagerly to see the narrow (and crooked) path she had carved from our steps to the sidewalk and the even narrower path across the front of our house on the sidewalk itself. It was quite an accomplishment for a small girl, to say nothing of the pile of snow she had also joyously scooped up to play in. All this was done in a hurry before big brother came home from Scout meeting, since he and his dad shared the snow-shoveling honors.

Sara sighed. "Now I know why everyone gets tired every time they shovel. Boy, is it hard work to make a path in that snow!"

Being willing to share responsibility with others is also vital in everyday situations. We found this could be worked out through responsibility for a pet, in our case a canary. For a time it was big sister's job to care for the bird. Later, she and Sara took turns at it. It was interesting to see how Sara consciously imitated her sister's attitudes and efforts and tried to fill the water and seed cups just as she had done. Sara was pleased to have this responsibility in the home.

This made us realize that, by chance of circumstance, we almost hadn't asked Sara to do much. Her older sister was a past mistress at shopping, taking mail, even escorting Sara to town for various errands. It was a temptation not to ask Sara to do much because there was an older child available.

Growth through responsibility is more than a catchall phrase that sounds good. It works.

Besides valuable experience, Sara gained much in characteristics needed as a grown-up: pride in a job well done, independence of thought and action, understanding of the jobs of others, and sharing in the family, to name only a few.

Doormat
or Dictator?

Both the retiring child and the bossy
one can learn valuable lessons as they grow

Some children seem tied to passivity, are nonresisting and retiring. Others not only demand their rights, they are downright bossy. Is one characteristic better than the other for your child or mine? And is either necessarily fatal for the total personality that will emerge later? The answer is no, provided real illness does not exist. But examination of both characteristics should be helpful.

There is a thin line between the naturally shy child who is also self-possessed and the retiring child who is trampled on by other children. Bravo for the child of the first type, who is endowed with a quiet personality and yet will still stick up for his rights.

Dick was one such fourth-grader. Though he stayed closer to home than some children and often preferred reading to playing, still it was obvious that he was free in a group. Other children sought him out, and even his disdain for a good fistfight proved no detriment.

"You're afraid!" challenged his father, who was secretly worried lest his son lacked courage.

Dick shook his head. "There's just no use in fighting," was his reply.

But for every Dick there is a Jim who isn't so successful.

"Bah! Bah!" Hearing the taunts, Jim's mother hurried to

the door. Her son, beleaguered and near tears, practically bumped into her. A coterie of boys, swarming up the sidewalk, suddenly dispersed as the house door opened.

"They took my book!" cried Jim. "They're always taking things. And Jack joggled my elbow today at school—on purpose. Made me spoil my math paper."

Torture for girls is more refined, but still hurtful. Sally's mother found her moping in her room one Saturday morning. "They won't let me help," was her excuse.

"They?"

"The kids. It's a puppet show. We're having it for the little children on the block."

"Did you ask to help?"

"No-o-o, not exactly. But they could let me if they wanted to." The last words rushed out.

It's all very fine to explain in adult terms that this is not the best way to meet life; that people have to learn to stand up for their rights, as in Jim's case, and to speak up for what they want, as in Sally's; that those who don't are left behind. But it's a long, slow process for some children to develop this concept.

Lacking ready-made ability to make himself or herself heard and felt, a child of this type may retreat from these unpleasantries. This is usually the "good" child, satisfying to adults if not to the children. Thus, to avoid trouble, this child becomes virtually a doormat, in the sense that he or she rarely speaks up in a group. At school he doesn't insist on the game he likes or the book he wants. He doesn't compete for line captain or helping jobs. If teasing and cruelty ensue, he hides or runs to Mother or the teacher.

There may be several valid reasons why this happens. The fact is, this child is probably either honestly retiring or shy by nature and sees little use in being "pushy" any more than Dick saw use in fighting. Or this child may be one of those who develop more slowly and just isn't physically or mentally ready to be more aggressive. It is often even possible that he may not have the rugged constitution of livelier friends.

Another type of temperament is also prevalent. Your child may be taking life too seriously, attaching undue importance to each rebuff. This sensitive child may also be more than normally affected by unfamiliar situations which, as growth occurs, must be met more and more alone.

Whatever the reason, as soon as you, as a parent, realize that your child is one of the retiring ones, being stepped on at will, you will be searching for ways to bolster him. Notice the word is "bolster"—not "change." Recognize his quiet nature for what it is, expect him to remain himself, but try to help him learn techniques for better relationships with people.

Keep your child away from group play for a while, to see if being with just one person (not the bully type!) will help him in learning to speak up. Without telling your child, enlist some friendly mothers whose children may play with yours. If the children are to be in your home, keep your ears open to see how play is going, but don't throw your weight around with them just because your child doesn't. (However, step in when playmates are flagrantly unfair.) And if an honest fight finally occurs, realize that this is a sign of progress. A certain number of these are inevitable, especially among boys.

Above all, treat the problem with a lot of lightness and hopefulness. If your child thinks you are bowed down and that you feel this is so serious he may never come out of it, he won't be able to carry his burdens at all.

But perhaps the best treatment is an oblique one. While you wait for your children to grow, learn, and develop, do what you can to build their self-confidence. Look into your own heart to see if you have contributed to undue dependency; if so, correct it. Likewise, give honest praise. Prepare each child for new situations ahead of time. Think up jobs to do. Increase their responsibility in going to the store, in helping with younger brothers and sisters.

Your child's schoolteacher will also be glad to cooperate. One child was boosted immensely when urged by his mother (at the teacher's instigation) to take a home-done chemistry experiment to school and explain it to the class. Look for ways not only to build your child's confidence but to have him portray his more desirable traits to friends.

But what of the child who, on the other hand, is always on the top of the heap, probably gouging those underneath? You certainly know the bossy, aggressive youngster; perhaps you have one in your home. Whereas the doormat child may be unnoticed, this one never is. He makes his own press releases, so to speak, and they are not always favorable.

Yet it is well to keep in mind that there are two kinds of aggressors. One, really smart and knowledgeable, is aggressive because he senses a better way to do things. Thus, there is reason behind his striving for his own way. In one sense this type is displaying early leadership and maturity. This is the rare child who will probably always be adjusted.

The other type of aggressor, sad to say, is oblivious to the relationships in a group. However, he has learned that he can get his way, sometimes by sulking, sometimes by using brute force.

Frequently the bossy one, finally "told off" by friends of the same age, resorts to playmates of a younger age level. Flattered at first by attention from someone older, these youngsters easily fall into the trap. Mr. or Miss Bossy directs everything, plans all the games, sends youngsters hither and yon on errands, swaggers home at night like a king or queen to the palace.

What the bossy child is really doing is trying to get a message across: "Look at me! I'm big and strong and wonderful." But in his heart he doesn't believe this. To further publicize the elusive idea, he may also talk about it out loud.

The other children branded Bobby, for example, a "liar." Listen to the stories he tells, they sniffed. What were these stories? Whenever someone displayed a new coat, a new pet, a new toy, Bobby immediately insisted he already had a bigger, better, or more expensive one!

Psychology tells us that the bossy child is probably insecure. He or she may be assertive because of feeling unwanted, or because domination over other children helps a sagging self-respect, or because frustration simply has to explode. This child has a core inside that won't allow giving in to others.

Parents may contribute to this without realizing it. Rebelliousness against adults may pop out as domination of peers.

What does the bossy child need? The same things all children need—love and understanding, only a bit more of both. Besides this, this child needs a good dose of firmness. It is no use letting him think that bossiness is justified.

No matter how gratified this youngster may feel when easy-going children kowtow rather than risk trouble, or when children bow to his every wish because he may have an attractive physical personality, bossiness can only lead to loneliness later and, in a sense, to dictatorship. By the middle years this child should be able to see that a few close friends with whom there is give-and-take on equal terms are better than any number who are controlled through bullying. Also he should see that play with the same age-group is more satisfying.

Sometimes the bossy child is also the spoiled child. You, as a parent, would do well to assess your own part in this behavior. Is there really any basis for the child's arrogance or insecurity?

Keeping the bossy child busy and interested is likewise important. The period between fourth and sixth grade is a fine time for this, a time when many hobbies emerge, when children love to collect things, and are fascinated with reading about cowboys, inventors, national heroes, careers. They love having pets, digging a garden, building forts, peering through a telescope, organizing nature clubs, going swimming, fishing.

Both the shy child and the bossy child can profit from cultivating an area of excellence that will bring others clustering around. The child who thus feels at ease within can graciously give in to others. He has no need to prove himself through bossing. He knows he is good!

Also, a child's peer group can do much as a catalyst to change bossiness into more acceptable behavior. Most children in the middle grades have developed a rather well ingrained sense of fairness. Knowing what is right, they are quickly ready to impress this on one who violates the code. "Letting nature take its course" with the child who is bossy with other children sometimes cures more quickly than anything parents can say. The child must learn that genuine leadership is considerate of others, whereas aggressiveness must be controlled to be helpful.

Thus the retiring child and the bossy child—potential doormats and dictators—learn valuable lessons during the middle years. By the end of the sixth grade your child knows the ground rules and, if you are lucky, will have outgrown the most bothersome of these characteristics. But if not, there is still learning time ahead to uproot immature reactions. One day you may be surprised to find someone praising your retiring son or daughter for "quiet strength" or your bossy one for "forthright leadership." Then you will know you were wise not to try to overhaul this personality completely when the basics of these traits were just emerging.

Children need our help. With it they grow and develop rightly. But we must often be patient for this to occur under God's good plan.

That Positive Approach

It is no longer "cute" when your growing child begins to imitate your worst habits

I remember the time when our son Bruce, as a tiny boy, stooped down by his tricycle and, with a small pair of pliers, began to tinker with the wheels.

I remember, too, watching him fondly, the small tawny head bent so earnestly over his task, and saying: "See, he's imitating his daddy working on the car. Isn't it cute the way children imitate the things we do?"

Looking back on the incident now, I'm not sure "cute" was the word for it. Experience has since taught me that there are more angles to this child-imitates-parents business than meet the eye. As a dear old friend sums up her opinion of it succinctly: "One of the most important things about bringing up your children is the example you set for them. You'll find that they invariably copy what you do."

Copy they do! I imagine there's scarcely a dad anywhere who hasn't had to alter his language because his children began to use the same slang he did. And all of us are aware that our fears are imparted to our children.

It may seem easy here to avoid setting the wrong example. What concerns me are less tangible attitudes.

If I say over and over that I detest housework and that it's pure drudgery to me, should it surprise me if neither of my daughters looks forward to keeping house?

If, after accepting a volunteer job, I keep complaining that it takes too much time and that I wish I didn't have to do it, is it any wonder my children begin to take a dim view of doing for others?

If I find fault out loud about most folks I meet or work with, will it be any wonder if my children learn to look for the bad things about people instead of searching for their good qualities?

Of course I don't really express negative thoughts like these. Or do I? Actually, I learned, when a spell of illness laid my spirits low, that the results were distressing indeed!

For example, one day while I was ironing, Sara, age five, was playing nearby. Although I was dimly aware that Sara was chatting to her doll, I didn't really listen until her words made me listen. Sara's voice broke in upon me, and might have been my own voice as she said: "It's hard to dress you when I'm so tired, dolly. Sometimes I don't see *how* I'll get through the day."

"Why, Sara!" I cried in shocked tones, nearly scorching a tablecloth in my dismay.

Later, I had to listen to my older daughter Jane repeating words of mine to much the same effect. Just home from high school, she dropped into the rocking chair by my desk for a chat.

"Oh, dear," she sighed, her usually happy face glum, "it was a horrible day at school. Just like a lot of days you have here at home, Mother."

Hearing this, do you wonder that I didn't meet her glance? Instead, I ostensibly became very busy at my typing. Was my face red! It was so patently evident where my daughters had learned their words. Yet if there is one thing I always say I want, it is for my children to accept their day-to-day duties with grace and lightheartedness.

Apparently I wasn't doing a good job of accepting life with grace and lightheartedness myself. That's what I mean by saying these attitudes are intangible. Despite good intentions, they sneak up on you. Saying that I'm tired one day doesn't mean much. But if I maintain an attitude of not being able to carry my burdens day after day, that's different. Gradually I set a pattern without being aware of it. My children not only absorb these patterns now, they are likely to go right on following my example when they're grown.

How to avoid this? The solution I turned up is deliberately to substitute positive attitudes for negative ones. I resolved every day to do three things with a positive approach: to find something to laugh about, something to sing about, and something to do for somebody else. This program leaves little time for spasmodic complaints and dissatisfactions.

A simple prescription? Yes. And easy to follow.

I find it's fun to search for things to laugh about around our house. And finding them makes it that much more fun to be alive.

Like when Sara knocked her milk glass onto the kitchen floor. Obviously it was an accident. So, biting my tongue to still my first horrified reaction to the mess on my clean linoleum, I laughed instead. "Look at that silly milk," I said brightly. "If we don't hurry and catch it, it will turn into a regular lake."

Sara, who had looked shocked at her clumsiness and then frightened at what I might do, relaxed and laughed too. "I'll help you, Mother," she said cheerfully, and forthwith knelt down and began to mop.

"It does look silly, doesn't it?" she added, giggling with her inimitable little-girl giggle. "This spot looks like a clown's head, doesn't it, Mother?"

If it did, the resemblance was remote. And I admit that what I had said was no great shakes at humor either. But the way I said it was what counted, that and my willingness to laugh at what couldn't be helped anyway. Thus a lunch hour which might have been spoiled by crossness went merrily on its way.

Or, like the time Sara and Bruce fell to squabbling, one of those brother and sister quarrels that come every so often in families.

Turkeyfoot Reading Center
Confluence, PA 15424

"Mother, make Sara leave me alone," yelled Bruce, age eight.

"I'm not hurting him." Sara defended herself loudly.

Since there was no way then to determine who was really at fault, I chose to treat it lightly, while gently but firmly moving Sara away.

"Come on, Long John," I admonished Bruce (we had just finished reading *Treasure Island* together). "Don't look so upset. We pirates have to keep our heads under fire."

Then to Sara, whose face was contorted with anger— "What a funny face you're making. Let's go see it in the mirror."

When we arrived at the mirror, Sara and I had a contest to see who could make the funniest face. Hearing our laughter, Bruce joined us, and ultimately big sister, and even Dad. Finally, there the whole family was, laughing together.

As for singing, did you ever try to complain when you sing? It can't be done, as I learned early.

When I was in high school I made a rule for myself: sing two songs before breakfast. I've forgotten the reason for this, but I know if a person sings right away after awakening, it sets a good tone for the day.

Early in my married life I employed a maid who always sang at her work. I know from experience how warm and friendly a house becomes when someone is singing in it. Now when I break into song, often it's because I'm consciously trying to give my day a lift.

As for mood, the type of song chosen can determine that. Personally I love the hymns, such as the familiar lines of "Jesus, Saviour, Pilot Me," "Rock of Ages," and "Faith of Our Fathers." Nothing calms me more quickly than the hymns; they bring peace to my heart and fill me with a sense of well-being.

On the other hand, folk and cowboy songs have their virtues, too, as Bruce would be quick to point out. It is through his influence that I am able to warble "Home on the Range," "The Big Rock Candy Mountain," and others. Jane encourages me in current popular songs, though in taste I remain old-fashioned.

Finally, in our family with three children, it's not hard to find deeds to do for others. As a wife and mother with full care of everything about the home, that is about all my job amounts to. However, there is always the time when the job goes stale on me, when I see my duties only piecemeal, and feel weighed down by them rather than inspired.

That is the time to seek out extra things to do for the children so that in doing them I may feel my own worth. Each day can become more special for me with the knowledge of the happiness I have brought to someone else, while the other nagging little duties assume their true proportions.

Besides, when I grow too occupied with washing, ironing, and cleaning, I sometimes overlook the human side of my job.

Perhaps something I heard Sara and one of her friends discussing sums it up best of all.

"I hate rain," said Donna, the friend. "I have to wear rubbers, and it makes the day dark."

"I love rain," said Sara. "It's fun to walk in puddles, and the rain makes the trees grow and the grass greener."

While they were talking, it was still raining!

What they said about rain didn't change the weather, but it did affect how they felt inside. I find, when I take a positive approach to my days, I feel better both outside and inside. And since what I as a parent say and feel is copied by my children, it's up to me to keep my outlook as bright as I can.

Besides, I'm convinced that, with God's help, all things in life can be borne, worked through, and conquered. It's most important that, through my attitudes, I build this sort of awareness for my children now.

Health Habits
Are Wealth Habits

**We fail with our children if we train
them in good physical health habits
and don't help them develop
a mental attitude of faith**

Our baby-sitter was chuckling when my husband and I came
home after our evening out. "I had your little fellow in bed
and thought he was asleep when he called me and made a big
fuss about getting up again," she related. "Seems we'd forgotten to brush his teeth. He scolded me, 'Mimi, teeth! teeth!' He
had to brush his teeth."

Well, that was when our son was a "little fellow." I can
only hope that he is as faithful about brushing his teeth today
as he was then. Still, I believe the habit is there.

Training our children in good health habits is one important facet of growth. I can remember my mother saying that
her prayer for me as a baby was that I would have good
health. I'm not sure that this doesn't sound a little old-
fashioned now. Perhaps modern parents attach more importance to having a child on the school honor roll, or captain
of the football team, or a potential president of some company.

But the fact remains that life is pretty restricted without
physical health and its concomitant of healthy growth. Or,
let's put it this way: While many accomplishments such as
those mentioned are possible in spite of poor health (and
many of the physically handicapped do rise superbly and
triumphantly above their handicaps), the person with a good

physical background has a body that works well, and everything else that is undertaken is just that much easier.

As I see it, the physical good habits that we can give our children have to do with three areas, no one more important than any other. Yet, in general, any one *without* the others is inadequate. These three areas are food, exercise, rest.

I think we all know what foods our children need; and certainly nowadays, with the advice of a pediatrician, we give babies all the food elements and more. But as a child grows older, maintaining a balanced diet becomes more difficult. "I don't *like* spinach," is one of the "jokes" we hear repeated, but it's more than a joke. We have a sort of unwritten clean-plate club idea at our house, but still my children tell me: "Mother, you plan the foods you like. *You* don't have to eat what *you* don't like!" And my little girl might add, "I can't wait until I'm a mother; then I won't serve any foods for dinner that I myself don't like to eat."

Well, it's not true that I plan meals with my own palate in mind. But I have tried to include a variety of foods in the menu that are palatable and still good for us.

At our house we settle on taking three bites or five bites or "x" number of bites of a food that's detested. Not all disliked foods have become liked, I'm sure; still, I have hopes that some have become tolerated.

Though it takes effort, it's also quite possible to discourage snacking on junk food between meals. To make up for this it's often a good idea to go on a planned popcorn or cookie spree some evenings.

Exercise is the second facet of good health habits that help growth. I, for one, have been cutting out those charts from the papers which say: "Test your child on these simple exercises. If he can do all of them, he's in top shape; if he can do only half, he's slipping; if he can do only a few, he's falling apart!"

Exercise is not something we can put before our children like food. Sometimes it just "happens," as with the younger child who is always running and playing. Later it becomes

more planned, and for many children who are not in orga-
nized sports such as basketball, volleyball, and such it comes
only in the summer when they can be outdoors.

My children are not athletes, but I have found there is
usually one area in sports which can be found to interest each
particular child. With mine it has been swimming, with the
addition occasionally of bowling. Other than that, I'm a great
believer in walking.

"But who walks anywhere anymore?" one of the children
remarked to me on that subject. And she was so right. Hardly
anyone does. A member of a school board said to me anent
the school bus situation: "You should hear the fuss we get
from the parents about buses. They don't want their children
to walk any distance at all, yet you know that these same
parents walked great distances to school!"

Have you ever thought of refusing your child a ride to the
library or to the store or to the post office, saying instead,
"Walk!" My son had a paper route and most people remarked, "How fine; it teaches him self-reliance," or, "It's
nice for him to earn his own spending money." But I also list,
as one of the values, the walking—yes, even when the
weather is bad.

With a little thought we can always encourage some form
of exercise for children, and remember that while many
forms cost money, walking is free! There can be badminton
courts in the backyard, a jungle gym for younger children,
and bars and basketball hoops for older ones. Digging in the
garden, shoveling snow, even cleaning one's room provide
both exercise and—glory be—some help for Mother and
Dad.

But good food and plenty of exercise are of no avail if a
child is tired all the time. Plenty of sleep is also a must. And
it's possible that you'll find, just like eating the right foods
and walking to school, going to bed early is something that's
no fun, either.

How much sleep a child requires is a moot question. Some
seem to need more than others. Some continue taking naps

up through kindergarten; others go off naps at about age three. I know one girl who had a nightly bedtime of nine thirty all through college. Others, however, seem to thrive on little sleep.

The amount of sleep for the growing child? This is something that each parent can work out by observing the child. One mother reports she figures generally on the amount of sleep "the book says" a child should have, and then ups it or reduces it according to the way the child responds. If her son drags out of bed in the morning, she puts him in earlier at night. If he is up ahead of the family, bothering everyone with his energy, she tries to put him in later at night.

But rest is more than sleep. The growing child is not too young to learn to vary his activities a bit in order to live in a relaxed fashion. This will help him when he grows up! "Change of pace" is important—taking a break in the middle of a hard studying stint and coming back to it refreshed, dropping out of a strenuous game for a bit to catch one's breath, a quiet time before bedtime so sleep will come quickly.

Food, exercise, rest—these are the areas where we can help train our children for good physical growth. Other health habits involve the care of our bodies: brushing teeth plus regular trips to the dentist, taking baths, washing hair, proper care of the feet and fingernails and toenails, good posture, and so on. Certainly decayed teeth affect health; callused feet make us hobble; neglect of any part of our bodies has an effect one way or another on health.

It's up to us to give our children every opportunity to have the finest physical growth possible. And every habit formed in childhood and carried over into a healthy adulthood is rarely completely lost.

But to me that isn't all. Maybe most people wouldn't put a belief in God as a final essential for good physical health. But I do. It seems to me that we fail with our children if we train them in good physical health habits and yet don't help them to develop a mental attitude of faith. For we know now through the study of what is called psychosomatic medicine that our thoughts affect our bodies.

When I was younger I tried to gather rules for living from the great philosophers and others who had written on the subject. I soon had a notebook full of maxims numbered 1, 2, 3, and on through the hundreds. And then during college my father wrote me a letter and said in it the one small phrase instilled in his mind by his parents and their parents and all those others who lived in our once-simpler world: Trust and obey.

The pitfalls for our children, it seems to me, are in learning to make decisions, to cope with disappointments, to discover how not to worry unduly. Certainly the means of learning is through prayer and asking for guidance. And the attitude is willingness to do God's will. Or, in other words, trust and obey God.

This I hope I can impart to my children. For what they think and believe they will become, and their physical health will stand or fall on that.

"Nobody Likes Me!"

Wise guidance from parents can take the sting from a child who feels friendless

Once upon a time there was a boy who was always the last to be chosen when the other boys were choosing sides for games. He decided, therefore, that no one liked him, and he always remembered not being chosen. This stood out much more clearly in his mind than many of the happy things that happened to him as a child. When he was grown, deep in his mind was always the thought, "People don't like me," even though he then had many friends. He could look back and realize that probably his being the last chosen in games was due more to his size and lack of coordination than to any basic character defects. Yet, to this day, the man has never been quite able to persuade his subconscious that people truly do like him.

A fairy story? No indeed! This sort of thing happens every day. The desire to be liked is one of the most universal human characteristics, and what happens to us in our childhood always colors our sense of worth.

It is likely to be the sensitive, shy youngster who has more trouble with being liked than the completely outgoing one. I remember watching two ten-year-olds of these two types. Both of them were eager to see a litter of new kittens at a home several blocks away. The outgoing, friendly child went right away, without being asked. Mary felt instinctively that people liked her, wanted her around. But Sue, the shy one, waited for an invitation, tortured in turn by her great desire to see the kittens and the uncertainty of whether she would be welcome.

A youngster of Sue's nature is also apt to count valentines she receives in the school valentine box and to feel that those who didn't send to her don't like her. When others gang up on her and leave her out, as children so often cruelly do, life is in ashes.

What we as parents say and do about such happenings may make the difference between their being accepted reasonably or becoming lifelong tragedies. Overemphasis and petty indignation on our part about these transient occurrences only make Sue feel that she was right, that people really don't like her. But if we take each happening sensibly, we can help her.

There are a couple of points of view that would help Sue if she feels that the boys and girls don't like her. One is to put this fact in its proper perspective. In actuality, Sue's "nobody" probably means "not everybody." If so, you might proceed like this:

"Do you like everyone in your room, Sue?"

Probably she will hesitate and then reply, "Well, pretty much."

"But aren't there some you like better than others?"

"Ye-es, I guess so."

"Well, then, not all people like you the same amount. You have some really close friends, and actually, as long as you are honest and aren't a pest to people, no one will dislike you. But in a large group there are always some we are not so friendly with, just because we don't know them well enough."

From this point it is easy to go on to the next if Sue still feels that she should have more friends. We can point out that if she wants Joe and Bill and Helen as friends, she will have to *be* friends with them, to make a habit of talking to them and treating them in a consistently friendly way. If she doesn't feel like doing this now, perhaps someday she will.

Meanwhile, she can enjoy the small group in which she does feel at ease.

Even in grade-school years, not being universally liked causes problems in the area of social life. In the early years, "birthday children" usually invite all their classmates to their party. But in the period between the fourth and sixth grade, the list becomes selective. And just around the corner lies junior high, where the heartbreak of not being in *the* social set is pretty terrific. To combat this, at least one suburban school has established the policy of discouraging private parties and encouraging several at school, to which everyone is invited. But in the meantime, your Sue and Jim may be suffering because suddenly, in fifth grade, they find they are not included in the cozy little gatherings that are going on in the homes of their acquaintances.

This involves a ticklish problem for parents. There are two ways to approach it: the first, through the other children and their parents; the second, through your own child. Personally I'm no believer in interfering either with other parents or with children in such an instance.

I know one mother whose child was omitted from a party list and who took it upon herself to phone the mother of the young hostess to ask why. Not everyone can be invited to every party, and in this case the omission didn't mean much more than that. However, the child involved was not one of the more popular ones. By such a phone call, the mother only placed undue emphasis on her child's lack of popularity and revealed the child's insecurity and her own. Besides, it made the other mothers and children wary of their relationships with this family, for word gets around about such things, and this made it harder than ever for the child.

So often, if you can hold your tongue, matters work out on their own. Wise guidance of your own child and developing in your own heart a philosophical approach to the fact that your child is not Mr. or Miss Popularity will help. Parents can sometimes be more anxious about a child's successful social life than the child is.

Sometimes you can do a bit of wise entertaining. The party should not become the occasion for either snubbing or catering to the children who have overlooked yours. Let the party become first of all an opportunity for your own children to have a good time with the friends with whom they are already comfortable. Perhaps a few others who are quite likely to accept a gesture of friendship should also be invited. These affairs do not have to be formal! Helping your home to get the reputation of being a place where people have a good time together is constructive and is not interfering.

Sometimes a child's lack of wide social relationships with other children can be remedied. Sometimes it cannot. And it is well for a child to begin to try, with parental help, to develop a philosophy to meet it.

All through the early years there is much difference in both physical and mental development among children. Along about sixth grade some begin to shoot ahead physically very rapidly; others lag behind and remain immature for several more years. So often, lack of social approval at this point is due to immaturity, not to any overt action of the child. If your child is one of the laggards, it is well to point it out to him or her. "Your turn will come—a little later!" But don't make this a theme song. Many a child has thought in his heart, though in his own words, "Methinks that Mother doth protest too much!"

Let Sue or Jim keep on trying to be friendly in all contacts, and, if that doesn't work, realize that life doesn't end or become useless because of their not being in "the gang." Perhaps Sue has talent, such as in music, or Jim is on the way to becoming a good athlete. Encourage these other outlets for their own sakes, not as ways to conform socially and earn acceptance. How many of us while growing up were encouraged to "learn to play popular music" as a key to party popularity, only to find ourselves remaining on the piano bench!

Many children who are slow in maturing, shy, and withdrawn will someday emerge as well-rounded adult personalities, interested in their work and interesting to others. This will be particularly true if their parents do not make an idol of peer-group popularity when they are young.

But in this world there are also children who are completely objectionable to other children. When they say, "Nobody likes me," they really mean no one! These are children who must change if they are to find acceptance now or later.

The parent of a child who is not accepted by peers should always try to find out why the child is really outside the pale. The schoolteacher may be of great help by telling you what sort of personality your child shows in school.

The parents of a certain child who never brought home any friends asked his teacher for clues and found, to their surprise, that the boy was constantly teasing and fighting. He was like a mosquito buzzing around the other boys, always tormenting them. No doubt he was seeking attention, but certainly not in the right way! He needed parental advice (sometimes punishment after a fight) to straighten him out. Of course, this child, too, needed to feel more secure; so the remedy had to be double-barreled—wise guidance and reprimand on the one hand, more praise and building up on the other.

If a child's antisocial behavior at school is extreme, do not hesitate to seek counseling. It may well be that some feeling of being rejected at home has led to an "I'm no good" attitude. Such a child "asks for" the cruel treatment by other children in numerous subtle and obvious ways. Perhaps we are the ones who need to be helped to a larger perspective.

Actually, there is probably no single answer to the complex problem of feeling that "they don't like me," because youngsters are so different and the reasons for feeling not liked are so many. Almost always a parent has to grope to find out how to help. The first duty, if the child is normal emotionally and has some likable qualities, is not to be anxious if the child's popularity is not widespread.

For some children who seem to have the gift of effortlessly being liked and of liking, there is no problem. Many youngsters, lacking maturity and feeling the need for more social approval, still seek for an understanding of the ways of being liked and need parental help.

No matter which category your own child is in, you will want to help him or her see that how many friends one has is not nearly so important as being able to forget oneself and enjoy others without tallying up the score. Thinking of others and their need to have a friend is also important. Friends are not to be counted, like stars on a chart. Friends are to be enjoyed.

Our Little Undependables

By setting a good example of dependability, we can help children want to be dependable too

"How would you like to come to my room after school and help me?" When Mrs. Mac, their beloved first-grade teacher, suggested this to Mary and Jane, now third-graders, they were delighted.

"We'll be there!" they sang out in unison.

And "there" they were in the first-grade room promptly after school that day, feeling grown-up and responsible, helping to straighten puzzles and activity projects as Mrs. Mac instructed them, setting up new projects for the next day.

This lasted for a few days. Then suddenly Mary came home after school on time. "How does it happen you aren't helping Mrs. Mac?" her mother asked.

Mary shrugged.

Her mother pursued it. "Did Mrs. Mac tell you not to come?"

"No."

"Did you tell her you weren't coming?"

"No."

"Well—"

"Jane isn't going," Mary burst out. "I don't want to go if Jane doesn't go."

"You should," said her mother. "You said you'd go. That's not being dependable."

"Depend-y-what?" asked Mary.

In thinking about dependability, I began wondering myself how to explain its mystery to a child. Put it this way for our purposes—*dependability means doing what you say you will do.*

Obviously, both Mary and Jane had failed to do what they said they would.

Force them, you say? Force a sulky child of six to eight to do something termed unselfish and a duty? You will probably get the overt act by dire persuasion, but you will not get the inner child. And you may encourage an opposite reaction when the next test comes along.

Besides this risk, there are reasons for the primary child to be *undependable.* We like to think of a person of good character as being dependable. But reliability or dependability requires a strong unified personality.

The young child has no such unity yet. There is a mercurial slant to his temperament. He quickly grows tired of doing things, as undoubtedly happened with Jane. Added to this, he has to have bolstering and support from his peers; he does not want to do anything his friends do not do, as happened with Mary.

Likewise, enthusiasms come and go. The next week, after their great enthusiasm about Mrs. Mac, Mary and Jane were bubbling over about putting on a puppet show. The next week it was something else. And such attention may wander no less from week to week than from hour to hour and minute to minute. Though most times a second-grader can be expected to be dependable in a job such as taking mail to the post office, I still remember one time when I watched our son stop to talk to a boy on a bike, go across the street to investigate a strange noise emanating from a garage, and pause to throw a few balls back and forth with a friend after depositing my letter gently on the grass. My worry accompanying this: Would he remember to pick up the letter again?

Thus, children are not natively dependable. This is a quality that must be nurtured and developed. We cannot expect too much too soon. But it does seem to me that dependability has been somewhat downgraded, and wrongly so, in our modern society. In general, integrity of purpose is not what it once was. Often people probably forget to do what they say they will. My grandmother always said, "Forgetting is no excuse," but we are not so stern in our pronouncements today.

How can we help a child to grow into dependability? Observe his serious concentration and interest in most requirements made of him. He truly means to be more dependable and does become so year by year, but his very immaturity often trips him up. And we cannot produce dependability by laying down laws.

We can lead a child's thinking. We can caution against agreeing to do a thing unless one means to do it. This is a form of good judgment that even some adults have not acquired. What about the woman who says she will provide cupcakes for a PTA meeting, and then doesn't do so? What about the man who accepts a committee chairmanship and then never even lifts his finger to do the job? Thus, if Johnny has a chance to run an errand for a neighbor, he should think it over and not say yes unless he means it. We parents can point out what saying yes implies. The decision about being dependable comes *before* the agreement, not after. We often forget this very important point.

Also, we can emphasize with Johnny the sometimes disastrous consequences of not being dependable. If he says he will feed big sister's parakeet while she is away on a visit, he can quickly understand that the parakeet may die if he neglects it. On the other hand, if Johnny means to be dependable and fails, we must always give him another chance. And we must never let him feel we do not still love him because of his failure. It's so easy to become angry and to lash out at a child for what we term "failings."

Johnny should also learn to expect to explain honestly if he cannot do something he has promised. For all of us, as humans, there come times when it is impossible to carry out an agreed-upon job. Expecting to explain as a matter of course will make it a habit later.

Another way we parents can help our young undependables is to set a good example. If I promise to make cupcakes for the PTA, I do not fail to carry through. If Dad promises to chair a committee at church, he does the job. We often excuse ourselves but, sadly, less often our children.

We should also keep promises not only to outside contacts but to the child especially. We all fall down on this now and then. We usually have reasons, like the time we promised to go to the zoo on Saturday, but Aunt Helen and her family came for dinner Friday night. By Saturday we were so tired and there was so much cleaning-up-after, we just forgot all about it. It all seems logical to us, but to the child it seems as if Mother just isn't very dependable about what she says she will do. And, like as not, Mother is too involved to explain.

Thinking carefully ahead of time before making promises will help. (This is what we are teaching Johnny, isn't it?) And further, explaining and apologizing for a promise broken is essential. (And we are telling him to do this too.) Never underestimate the importance a child places on dependability in you.

In fact, everything cracks up all around when a child thinks he cannot depend on his parents. Though he probably still does not know what the word means and cares less, he has to be sure that we are there and, above all, can be counted on. He may not realize either, with all our efforts, the importance of his being dependable, but he does know he must feel that we love him, his undependability and all.

It is as he sees in us this trait of dependability, and as we guide him toward it in his thinking and actions, that he will begin to want to be dependable too. Thus, someday, perhaps not in the primary years but later, the framework we have laid down now, outside the child, will move inside him. And on the day when the inner child wants to be dependable, the battle will be won.

Is Politeness
Out of Date?

The truly polite person follows the
Golden Rule—and that is never out of date

This happened on a crowded suburban train carrying shoppers home from a day in Chicago. Standing in the aisle next to me was an elderly lady, much stooped, with a number of bundles in her arms.

Sitting on the seat beside us were a mother and her high-school-age daughter and another woman who, I soon gathered, was the girl's teacher. How that girl did chatter on, trying to appear bright and sophisticated, and all to impress her teacher! In the meantime, however, the mother kept repeating in a low voice, indicating the old lady, "Helen, please let the lady have your seat." She tried at least half a dozen times to get Helen to do this. Helen merely ignored her.

Finally a young woman sitting nearby quietly offered her own seat to the elderly woman and ended the episode.

But I couldn't get Helen off my mind. Is politeness as much out of date as Helen's actions indicated?

I would hate to think so. Yet many young people, and even adults, behave as though they think it is smart to be rude.

Oh, I'll grant that certainly some acts, labeled polite, are outmoded. Men no longer give their seats to women, particularly when they return home from the day's work together. Men don't remove their hats for women in elevators anymore, either. In fact, men no longer treat women as frail and sheltered beings.

But this fact, far from making politeness passé, only gives it a broader application. Today the practice of good manners is equally important for girls as well as boys; for women as well as men.

This is the way I want my children to consider it.

Take the matter of Helen giving her seat to the old lady. That comes under the heading of doing for others.

It's not enough, to my way of thinking, to make the general rule for children—You should always give your seat to an older person. What, then, about the small boy with his arm in a sling who can't find a seat on the bus? Or the very young mother with her baby on one arm and parcels in the other who has to stand? Isn't there a better rule?—Always give your seat to anyone who needs it, regardless of age.

The same principle applies to helping anyone who needs help, whether it be carrying a heavy bundle, assisting with some job, or just picking up a dropped package. My young son (or daughter) is just as much obligated to help a pal his own age carry a bedroll down the street as he is to carry his grandfather's suitcase for him. Or to do any other thoughtful act for anyone of any age who needs it.

I hope when my young daughter offered to wipe the dishes for me it wasn't because she regarded me as such an old lady! But it was hot and I had had a busy day; she knew I was tired. I rather hope she thought of this when she suggested helping.

Politeness, then, means doing for others. It also means appreciation and thoughtfulness. Very often these can be expressed by using a few simple phrases such as thank you, please, excuse me, pardon me. Saying is admittedly easier than doing, yet how hard it is sometimes for children to remember.

There was the Halloween night when I accompanied my young daughter trick-or-treating. As she raced up to each house, pounded on the door, and breathlessly opened her sack for the treat that was forthcoming, it suddenly dawned on me. She was closing her sack and running away, without even saying, "Thank you."

And when it comes to saying, "I had a nice time," it also takes much coaching for children to get the habit. I had a discussion about this with my young son one day. A friend of mine was calling for him in the car to take him to a birthday party. "Remember to say, 'Thank you for the ride,' " I admonished him. "Then, when the party is over, tell them, 'I had a nice time.' "

My son wrinkled his forehead worriedly. "I think I can remember to say, 'Thank you for the ride,' because that will be only a minute from now," he remarked. "But saying, 'I had a nice time,' is such a long way away, I'm afraid I won't remember that!"

Yet young children with all their forgetfulness are eager to do the right thing and will learn if constantly reminded. With prompting, they will even eagerly write thank-you letters, with smudgy, ungrammatical gusto. It is usually when they are older and more blasé that they sometimes grow downright careless about the little phrases.

And all of us, at all ages, have trouble using the phrase *I'm sorry.* Admitting a mistake or wrongdoing is never easy. Yet, if we are truly thoughtful of other people, we never fail in this.

But besides doing for others and showing appreciation and thoughtfulness, politeness is something else. It is showing consideration for others. It is not doing something we might like to do—for the sake of others.

Perhaps this is the hardest area of all. At dinner, for instance, what difference does it make if our son uses a boardinghouse reach for the butter on the other side of the table; if our little girl stuffs her mouth full of peas and then, with a whishing noise through her teeth, starts to tell us a story; if all of us shovel our food in so rapidly you'd think we were hurrying to a fire?

No difference, really, as long as we nourish our bodies,

except that it's not considerate of other people to do these things.

It's not considerate of other people to walk in front of them, either; to barge out doors ahead of them; to bump them as you go by; to push ahead of them in line; or to interrupt when they are talking. And children can be shown early what consideration means by being trained to share toys cheerfully, to give their guests first choice in games, and to take turns, among other things.

Yes, this attitude of consideration, and particularly the lack of it, reaches out into many areas in our dealings with people. Yet, if enough children were taught at home the basics of consideration for others, some of this would clear up. Isn't this something for us to think about?

Sometimes I fear we parents are at fault, even with the best of intentions. We are so busy that we let some rudeness at home slip by. We sometimes fail to show our children what they ought to do and then are shocked when they don't do the right thing. And of course, children sometimes fail to understand some of the fine points at first.

One day when I was expecting guests I requested my son to come in after school and meet everyone. Imagine my distress at discovering, when he arrived, that he had his shoes off! All the time I was introducing him he was burrowing his sock feet self-consciously under the edge of the living room rug.

Later, when I told him how I felt he explained, "Coming home from school I got my shoes wet. You always tell me to take off my shoes at the back door when they are wet, so I did!"

Granted, it takes patience to make polite children, but it is worth it. Even though formality is out of date and the way we use politeness has changed, politeness itself is timeless. If Helen had only realized, she would have made a much better impression on her teacher if she had given up her seat to the old lady and let the conversation go.

No person, young or old, can go wrong in doing for others,

expressing appreciation and thoughtfulness, using consideration in life. This is another way of saying that a truly polite person follows the Golden Rule. The Golden Rule will never go out of date, and politeness of the right sort never will, either.

II

As Parents– We Need Understanding

Apply thine heart to understanding.
Proverbs 2:2 (KJV)

Does It
Really Matter?

Do we have tolerance and understanding for children in their world?

That morning, standing at my front window, I watched Sara, my four-year-old, at play. She was wearing sturdy corduroys, a gabardine jacket, and scuffed shoes. But her hands, busily guiding her tricycle, were encased in white, Sunday-go-to-meeting gloves! It seemed to my grown-up standards that the gloves made her look silly. I almost wished I hadn't given in to her insistence on wearing them.

But one look at her face reassured me. Sara's smile was absolutely delighted. Actually, though she would soil the gloves, they would wash. She would never go to enough dress-up affairs to wear them out before she outgrew them. Why not let her enjoy them?

Why not, indeed? As I went about my work the thought kept coming back to me. Why should I have considered not letting Sara wear the gloves? I had even argued with her about it. It was already established that damage to the gloves didn't matter.

What, then, about my thought that she would look silly? Look silly to whom? The trashman, perhaps; a few women on their way shopping; a neighbor coming to the front door for the paper. Would they really think her silly and what if they did? Did it really matter?

I decided it didn't matter that Sara wore white gloves to

play, except in my mind, and that it all came back to that troublesome, catchall phrase, "grown-up standards." Yet I realized that as a mother I all too often judge my young children's activities by grown-up standards.

Paul the apostle said it much better than any of us and in unforgettable language in his letter to the Corinthians so many years ago: "When I was a child, I spake as a child, I understood as a child, I thought as a child: but when I became a man, I put away childish things" (I Cor. 13:11, KJV).

In this verse Paul draws a sharp line between childhood and adulthood, each with its own interests and habit patterns. But don't we parents sometimes blur that line, actually treating our little children as though we wished they were small adults?

This thought carried me back to my own childhood and something that occurred when I was scarcely older than Sara. As it happened, this was about gloves also. I could still visualize myself as I must have looked then, on that special Sunday morning.

That was the morning when mother gave in to my impassioned plea to wear a pair of short white gloves to Sunday church school. Mother related that she was dubious about allowing me and that it was just as she had expected—I looked very odd sitting there with gloved hands in my lap, a bare expanse of arm shining between glove cuffs and short, puffed sleeves. But my face was absolutely beatific, I was so happy.

But there was another child there who was not so happy. Her mother came up to mine after Sunday school. "I see you let Mary Margaret wear her short white gloves today," this other mother said. She sighed. "I wish now I'd let Mildred wear her big new red hair ribbon as she begged to, even though the bow doesn't match her dress and I thought it too large."

Her voice trailed off. My mother looked at Mildred sitting primly and glumly on a chair, a proper small pink hair ribbon on her hair, but on her face a most unhappy expression accented by unhappy, rebellious eyes.

Now Mother's voice came back clearly to me in the words with which she was wont to end this story: "I always say when it comes to things like wearing rubbers or crossing the street, questions of health and safety, I can't give in. But on little things, things that matter so much to a child but may seem silly to me, I can give in—and I try to remember to."

It seemed to me a good time that very morning, with Sara playing in her white gloves, to take stock of my own self and see in what areas I might be forgetting to remember. Mainly it seems my children and I differ in three areas: about harmony in clothes, such as was typified in the glove incident; in a difference of opinion about what constitutes untidiness; and in a complete divergence of views on the way to do any job adequately.

Right before me, as I did a bit of morning cleaning, was a challenge to the tidiness theory. In the middle of Sara's room sat a crazy concoction of tables, pillows, and old blankets. She and her seven-year-old brother Bruce had informed me the night before that this was their playhouse.

"Don't you dare touch it, Mother," Bruce had warned.

Now, as I dusted, my hands itched to touch it, to tear it down and restore the room to a semblance of order. But my just-renewed tolerance for children in a child's world sustained me. For a day or two of pleasure for the children, the untidiness didn't matter. Besides, they didn't consider the room untidy; it looked fine to them.

It also always looked fine to Bruce when he "cleaned" his room, which he did periodically, by moving his trucks from side to side, transferring his books from one overloaded shelf to another, dragging his small desk about interminably. As far as I could see, his cleaning could just as well be done by opening the window and letting a high wind blow everything around. The results couldn't be any more chaotic.

But why argue about that, either? It doesn't matter. Bruce was happy. He thought his room improved by his efforts.

There are other areas in the untidy situation. I think it's pretty untidy business for children to slosh around in water whether in the kitchen sink or in a puddle in the yard. But it gives them a certain sort of gorgeous joy that few other activities can offer them. And what I call messy isn't messy to them.

And I certainly considered it untidy business to have Bruce bring home salvaged whipped cream containers, broken desk fixtures, and rusty coat hangers out of the junk piles we set on the street each month for village collection. This made me sigh and say, "Now where did you get that?" or even worse, "Oh, Bruce, you can't keep that, we have so much junk already!"

But this wasn't junk—not to Bruce at that moment.

Of course, there is a limit on this as in all such things. One can still be tolerant of young children and allow them to enjoy a child's life, without permitting them to "take over the place." A child also learns from give-and-take in a family, from having to consider the wishes of others, from having to conform to a family pattern. When company is coming, playhouses have to be torn down to make way for pleasure for Mother and Dad; playing in the sink doesn't have to involve splashing water all over the kitchen; and brother's junk pile doesn't have to grow so large that everyone else has to move out.

There are limits to "yes" as well as "no." Activities that are wrong or actually destructive must be restricted. But many small things that we adults think silly can be allowed and many a child's happiness added to by a little thought as to what is important. And how many parent-child battles can be avoided!

Also, my children and I differ as to when a job is done adequately. There was the time when Bruce gave a circus in our backyard. To me his plans sounded exceedingly vague, and yet he was asking the neighborhood children to pay a penny admission. I was tempted to intervene, to jack up the circus to what I considered grown-up standards. But, on second thought, I didn't.

And, of course, the children came and had a wonderful time doing what seemed to me practically nothing. It left me ruminating that what seems inadequate to grown-ups rarely seems inadequate to children. I was worrying about what the parents would think of their children not getting their money's worth. But how can we parents know for sure what a child considers his money's worth?

So it goes. And what could I tell my husband's boss and his wife, when they came to dinner, about that faded little bunch of dejected pansies which Sara had put in an honored place in the center of the hall table?

I could, of course, have picked the flowers for Sara (so the stems would be even, not broken off at different lengths), chosen the vase (so it would be my best silver one, not the gaudy, rose-colored one with the crack), and arranged the blooms (so they would have made an even pattern of color, not be stuck in the vase all higgledy-piggledy). Then I would have had a lovely flower arrangement for company dinner, which matters to me. But, at this point, should it matter? Is it as important as Sara having a child's joy in doing a job for Mother and surveying her very own vase full of flowers in a prominent place in the family picture?

Yes, I'm afraid many of us parents have too completely "put away childish things" to remember the joys young children receive from little things—from choosing their own clothes whether they match or not; from not having to be tidy like grown-ups; from playing with complete freedom. There are many other small and cherished projects that matter to them which need not matter so seriously to us parents.

Then and there I resolved to try harder to let my children be children while they can. Soon enough they become adults, hemmed in by conventions and other restrictions. All I have to do is to ask myself about their proposed activities: "Am I censuring this because of grown-up standards?" and "For a child, does it really matter?" If it doesn't, I can let them revel in the fun and freedom of childhood while they can.

And I can relax and enjoy their harmless whims with them.

Just as I finished thinking this, Sara was at the door pounding to come in. As I greeted her she pounced upon me, her face radiant. "I've still got my gloves on, Mother," she announced, holding up her two chubby hands. "They look so nice, Mother. I'm so glad I'm wearing white gloves today on my hands."

It's Doing Your Best That Counts

Children need to be judged for their own worth—not for how many A's are on the report card

When it was report card day at school my children thought up an experiment. Bruce was in seventh grade, Sara in fourth. "Let's get out my old fourth-grade report card," Bruce suggested, "and Jane's fourth-grade one (big sister, Jane, was now in college), and then compare them with Sara's."

When the three fourth-grade cards were laid side by side, I came over to look. I noticed immediately that Sara, currently, and Jane, a long time ago, had a good crop of A grades. "Why, Bruce," I said before I thought, "look at the girls' cards! Didn't you get any A's in fourth grade?"

"I guess not." Bruce pulled himself away from contemplation of the B's and C's on his card. From the disappointment on his face, I guessed he'd forgotten his grades, or he'd not have become involved in this. "Well, I make A's now, don't I?" he asked, suddenly defensive. He turned on me crossly. "That's all you parents talk about—A's, A's, A's!"

"But it isn't all we talk about," I defended myself to my husband later. "I've bent over backward to tell the children that grades aren't important."

"True," my husband said, "but underneath we all want our children to excel. Without realizing it, we let little things drop, just as you did with Bruce, giving them the feeling that A's do count."

Are you an A-grade (or E-grade, or whatever system is used in your school to indicate the top grade) parent? Do you worry because your child doesn't get all A's, or half A's, or maybe not any A's at all on his school report card?

One school official told me that on the day after report cards come out, the school office is deluged with phone calls from irate parents. Another teacher related, "Sometimes sad things happen on report card day." He recalled a time when a boy named Sam didn't leave after school, but kept hanging around, fussing with books in his desk. When the teacher finally told him he must go home, he burst into tears. "I can't go home," he sobbed, "I only have B's and C's on my report card, and my dad says I have to get A's. I just can't go home."

We parents like to think that most of us aren't that severe in our attitudes. But often we influence a child as this fifth-grader, Anne, was influenced. Her sister, in eighth grade, is always on the top honor roll. One day Anne asked her teacher wistfully, "Do you suppose I could ever get up enough steam to make straight A's too?"

"This wasn't Anne's idea," her teacher remarked. "Some grown-up gave it to her."

Yes, we grown-ups give our children ideas about grades. And because they take these so to heart, and build their attitudes from ours, we need to watch what we say and do about A's. We need to watch, first, about comparisons.

A friend told me that when her son, Larry, brought home a B in science, she inquired immediately, "What did Butch and Skippy get?" Then she related: "I was sorry as soon as I'd asked, because it turned out that Butch and Skippy got a B+ and an A. Then I realized that it doesn't have anything to do with Larry what anyone else gets."

So it was with me. Although my own children dreamed up the idea of comparing their report cards, I had no business stepping in with my remarks to Bruce. Comparisons between sister and brother, between your child and the boy next door, between your child and your own grades when you were in school, have no place in the picture. A child deserves to be judged on his own worth. He needs to compare this report card with his own previous record, not someone else's. A child should be encouraged to work at his own level, whether that makes him a top student, a medium one, or even a less-than-medium one. Children are born with different native capacities. One child can work best with his hands, another with his mind. If he isn't topnotch in study, you may be able to encourage him to pursue his interests or hobbies in which he does excel. But if each child does the very best of which he is capable, nothing more should be asked.

How do you find what your child's "best" is? Most schools have tests that indicate your child's abilities and generally what can be expected. So, what if your child tests out to have innate ability but is not making use of it? As parents our tendency is to grump around and begin to nag the child to do better. These expressions of impatience and frustration often fail to produce results, since there is another possibility to keep in mind. Your child could be one of the "late bloomers." Regarding grades, we need to watch, second, for the late bloomer.

"Late bloomer," a term considered contemporary, is probably much older and can be defined as referring to someone who finds his niche late in life. Or, for a child in the early years, it applies to the underachievers who haven't yet found the motivation to do well in school. Today when we parents fuss so much about grades we only reemphasize the modern admiration of precocity and don't give attention to potential for future growth.

There is no way adequately to predict when a late bloomer will reach peak performance. For instance, what about U.S. President Calvin Coolidge? We are told his "bud did not even begin to open until after college."

Granted, there is a good deal of uncertainty involved in knowing whether a child is a late bloomer, but it still seems that parents are well equipped to make a good guess at it. Parents have knowledge of family background, manners and mores, which, combined with instinct and love, can go a long way to ferret out what makes a child behave the way he does.

And motivation, which is not measurable, is so important. A child who is motivated by perseverance and effort sometimes appears to do even better than his best, all because he possesses this strong feeling about where he is going. Sad to say, parental nagging and expressed dissatisfaction with the way a child is doing in school never promotes motivation, either.

It's a narrow and precarious tightrope a parent has to walk: not to compare a youngster's grades with someone else's when A-grades are held in such esteem, and to be patient if a child is one who is slow to mature and may zoom along later in life, though not in the early years. Above all, we need to approach the matter of school grades with love and understanding. Tests or no, good grades or no, as parents we can believe in our child's potentialities. This faith in a child's potential is more important to him and to us than A's on a report card.

Today's world is so full of competitive efforts that our children are under pressures we never knew when we were growing up. One pressure we can remove, if we try, is the A-grade pressure. It may take some work on your part to look happy, and feel happy, for a less than A-grade report card. But it's one of the greatest gifts you can give your child —the feeling that you like and approve of him just as he is.

Rivalry Within
the Family

**Patience is needed to endure rivalry
in the family; also an understanding that
its expression leads to development
of self-esteem**

Following dinner one night I assigned our third-grade son to
the job of wiping some of the dishes, our kindergarten-age
daughter to clearing the table. Somewhat later I found Bruce
drying silverware, industriously counting as he laid each
piece on the kitchen table, "One, two, three, four—"

"Why count?" I wanted to know.

"I'm checking on the job Sara did and the one I'm doing,"
he informed me. He scowled. "I don't want to do *more* than
Sara."

This, in essence, is the story of sibling rivalry, whether it
is between brothers and sisters, brothers and brothers, or
sisters and sisters. All of us who have more than one child
know all too well that this rivalry exists.

Parents with young children see so much of it! The yelling
and arguing (yes, and sometimes actual nose-punching) seem
to continue interminably.

What kind of child is the youngster who experiences such
violent emotions in trying to keep up with or get ahead of his
brothers and sisters? We can only generalize, of course. Parents are the first to realize that no two children are alike and
that allowances must always be made for individual differences.

Studies show that the six-year-old wants his own way.

Also, he cannot bear to lose at games and will cheat if necessary to win. He is jealous of possessions of other children. The seven-year-old, although he is chiefly compatible with siblings, is also jealous of their privileges or abilities. He worries about his place in the family or school group. He may be jealous of his father's attention to his mother. The eight-year-old feels some jealousy of Mother and Father's being together. He is possibly less compatible with siblings than is the seven-year-old, likewise he is selfish and demands much attention.

Jealousy is a word—and feeling—that emerges in this listing and which applies especially to our problem.

We've all seen a mother sitting with a new baby on her lap. When this happens, it is not uncommon for a slightly older toddler to push the baby away and try to clamber up himself. Jealousy probably accounted for a dinner-table scene at our house.

Dad had just returned from a week's business trip. The chatter was noisy, as each of our three children tried to tell first and loudest what had been going on during Dad's absence. Finally our youngest raised her hand, just like a pupil. Asked what she wanted, she announced plaintively: "I want to talk. Daddy's not listening to *me.* "

Jealousy over parental attention is only one facet of family rivalry. There can be jealousy over friends.

Our next-door neighbor, Janis, a third-grader, most often played with Bruce, our third-grade boy. But sometimes, tiring of masculine games, Janis seemed to favor Sara, our kindergartner who had an array of girl's toys. Sara was quick to capitalize on this. When Janis was coming to play, Sara rushed to the front door before Bruce could, hinting slyly, "I can play with you, Janis." Or she answered Janis' phone call, suggesting, "Come see *me,* Janis." She was a tagalong when Bruce and Janis were playing.

"Leave us alone," demanded Bruce at times. "Janis is *my* friend."

"She's mine too," countered Sara.

"She's not!"

"Is too!"

"Not!"

Besides this strong tendency toward rivalry, young children are imbued with the competitive spirit that is also inherent and so much emphasized in our modern culture. As someone points out, a child often even competes with himself. Observe the boy alone tossing a ball tirelessly into a basketball hoop, or riding faster and faster on his bike, or even testing his lungs to see how loudly he can yell. More common, however, is competition between children.

We were staying at a hotel during vacation. When we got to our floor, Bruce and Sara practically knocked each other down trying to jump off the elevator first, then took off, running down the long, narrow corridor. The goal? Our hotel room door.

When Dad and I arrived, Bruce had the doorknob in firm grasp, was using his knee to push Sara away. "Give me the key," he implored his father. "Let me open the door. I got here first!"

"He did not. He tripped me," shouted Sara. "I get to open the door! Give me the key!"

Who knows who reached the door first? We never did find out—and this is only one of the dilemmas in which parents are caught.

Any mother could go on and on with illustrations of how this rivalry, stemming from jealousy and/or competition, is practically constant in young children. Although much of this is inevitable, there are many areas where parents can help.

It is all too true that sometimes one child in a family is favored. Instead, each child should *know* this: "Mother and Dad love me just as much as they love the others." Although this may not cure jealousy of a general nature, it destroys the cause for one important and devastating phase of it among those in a family.

But although love of parents can be equally dispensed,

privileges, gifts, rulings on arguments usually have to be tempered by the ages of the children in a family. Sometimes, from the child's point of view, these may seem grossly unequal. Somehow a parent has to try to compensate for these differences of age. It's something like giving a handicap in golf. Little sister isn't old enough to go to the store alone, but she dusts so well. This is the way she can help best today.

On the other hand, the older child who necessarily may have more freedom and activity must learn not to flaunt these before the younger one.

There are also differences in abilities to be coped with. The comparisons that slip out—"Why is it taking you so long to learn to skate? Your brother learned in no time!" or "Your sister never had trouble with math, what's the matter with you?" must die on the tongue and never be said.

How to teach a child to share with others, including his brothers and sisters, is another sticky question parents must try to answer, while at the same time defending a child's right to have a place of his own for toys and precious possessions apart from the other children.

Most parents, at this point, probably realize that it would take the wisdom of Solomon (or more) to do the job perfectly. They know that they must content themselves with trying hard to dispense justice and favors as fairly as possible. In the meantime, when the going gets too rough, "planned separation" may help to alleviate teasing and fighting (and do wonders for parental nerves!).

It could mean leaving little sister with a sitter while taking brother to a ball game; or busying brother at the basement workbench so that sister and her friends can play upstairs without interference; or using any reasonable means to keep children apart for a while until the smoke clears away.

In any case, parents can take hope that with age, jealousy —unless it becomes abnormal—is usually outgrown, and family rivalry dies down. Even though jealousy may seem to linger on mildly on a personal level, children soon begin to respond as a family unit. Big brother defends little sister from her tormentors; sister is proud when brother turns out to be the star of the Little League. Both unite to defend the family honor when someone questions their mother's talent in leading the PTA. At the same time, group competition, superseding individual competition, fosters unselfishness.

Probably the best help for parents is for them to realize that, annoying and undesirable as it may seem to adults, sibling rivalry in the early years is quite natural. In fact, the principle it represents is healthy. One of the earliest drives of a child is the necessity to attract attention to his own worth. Gradually, as he does this, first through unacceptable methods until he learns more acceptable ones, he comes up with a good, strong sense of self-esteem.

Hurry! *Hurry!*
HURRY!

In this day of tension we should respect —and protect—a child's slow, joyous manner of living

When I wakened early that summer morning it turned out to be dark and threatening. Thunder rumbled. Lightning flashed. And my young son was due on his paper route in fifteen minutes! Tumbling out of bed, I wakened Bruce, fumbled into my clothes, hurried out to help him deliver the papers before the storm broke.

His dad was out of town with the car, so we had to walk. I felt breathless with the hurrying, grabbing a paper, bustling up to a house door, depositing it inside the screen—all done against the wind. *"Hurry,"* I kept calling to Bruce. *"Hurry!"*

But did he hurry? No, not much. When I ran, he trotted; when I trotted, he walked.

When we arrived home again, I was breathless. And I began thinking about how much I'd nagged at Bruce, Hurry! *Hurry!* HURRY! Was it necessary? Goodness knows I'm always hurrying. But Bruce was only a little boy. He didn't feel much need of it yet.

After this incident I began to check on myself around home. Like other parents, I seemed to be always trying to keep my children on the move. In spite of the fact that I had seen article after article on the slow tempo of children, I always seemed to be too involved in grown-up business to remember.

There I was, trying to hurry seven-year-old Sara to finish her meals, even though I know that small children usually take longer to eat than grown-ups. And I was always hurrying Bruce on his Cub Scout projects. Hadn't he finished that scrapbook yet? Why, I thought he should have done it in half the time!

Yet I know that saying *hurry* to young children is rather futile, for they have little concept of time. I teach kindergarten children in church school. One little girl who had been ill and absent for a couple of Sundays told me solemnly, "I was absent *next* week."

Besides, when life is so wonderful and there are so many interesting things to do and see, why not take time to see and feel and experiment? I often told Sara to hurry home from school. One day she strolled in, inordinately late, and informed me happily that she had taken 145 steps between school and home. She knew, because she had counted them!

Parents of youngsters, from six to eight years, have a particular responsibility on this hurry business. In a sense, we feel our children aren't babies any longer. Thus, we lose sight of the fact that many of their reactions, though modified from babyhood, still have the same early roots of curiosity and interest, and they are far from ready to settle down into businesslike adulthood.

When our older daughter started first grade I was startled to discover how many times the teacher was keeping her after school. On inquiry it developed that it was not a disciplinary problem. "She's just young," her teacher explained with understanding. "She doesn't realize yet about getting her work done. She's wide-eyed with the wonder of school; she sits, taking everything in. So she has to stay to finish her work. Later, she'll not need to." This wise teacher proved to be right.

But even later, when this older daughter was in high school, she still had moments when she moved in slow tempo. I took her and one of her friends into Chicago for luncheon and shopping. Coming home, they were exhausted in the way of young girls. They drooped, their feet hurt, they dragged along. No matter what, I couldn't hurry them.

This relaxed attitude and slowness are only normal to youngsters of various ages. But do I let mine act their age? No, I must hurry, hurry them up!

Again there was Bruce and his "helping" with the dusting. He had his own original seven-year-old method of work. When he first went in to the living room he headed for the piano. He might dust a key at a time for a period, each key going *bong, bong, bong* as he hit it, then turn to rippling his dustcloth up and down the entire keyboard, making runs and trills like any maestro. It took him a long time to finish the piano and after that just any table or chair wouldn't do. He liked a large, open tabletop (our nest of tables was super) where he could rub and shine and rub over again.

Since his "dusting time" was usually before school in the morning, so much preoccupation with a couple of projects meant he didn't cover much else before the school bell rang.

One day I spoke sharply about it. "You'll have to hurry faster so you can finish. I need the whole living room dusted, not just—"

"I do hurry fast, Mother," he interrupted. "But this table was real dusty. Besides, there are smudges from someone's fingers all over it." His tone was injured. "You want me to get it clean, don't you?"

"Yes," I agreed. "But it doesn't have to be that clean. I could see you from the kitchen. You were rubbing a while and then you'd sit and dream a while and then you'd rub."

I broke off. I was suddenly appalled what haste and impatience had made me say. Bruce's face was hurt and indignant. "I just won't dust anymore for you," he said in an aggrieved tone. Then he added, "But I thought you liked my dusting. Yesterday you said you did."

I've decided it's time to drop that word "hurry" from my vocabulary. Besides, frequently when I've been running around shouting *hurry, hurry,* at my children, it's my own fault that they are under such pressure. A little matter of timing helps. Rather than giving them just enough time to do any job, I should start earlier, so they could move at their own speed to accomplish it. This applies to going to bed, getting up in the morning, homework, and all manner of matters.

After all, what are we all hurrying for, anyway? Where does it get us, besides making us tired?

The other day I stopped hurrying long enough to try to think this through. In quietness at my desk, I was able to bring the subject a bit more into focus. Children and adults alike, whoever we are, wherever we are, all have the same amount of time in each day. In a sense, ours is a stewardship of time. Time comes to us as a gift from God. Certainly the unhurried tempo of life for children is within God's plan. I like what Ecclesiastes 3:17 says: "God . . . has appointed a time for every matter, and for every work" (RSV).

In this day of tension we should respect—and protect—a child's slow, joyous manner of living as long as ever we can.

I try to stop and think now: Is it necessary to rush around so much? I'm surprised at the number of times it isn't. I've decided that good stewardship of my own time means relaxing once in a while, rather than packing every last second of my own days with mad activities.

I know that if I can relax more myself, it will be good for all of my family. On the paper route that rainy morning, if I hadn't been all tense and flurried, I wouldn't have ended up half so tired; Bruce and I would have accomplished just as much; and Bruce wouldn't have had to listen to me continually nagging, Hurry! *Hurry!* HURRY!

The Reason
Behind the Reason

**We shouldn't be so quick to label
a child's response as unreasonable or
stubborn. Often there's a deeper reason**

Our seven-year-old daughter and I had a spirited argument one day about her wearing slacks to school. It was rather cool, and she'd just had a cold. I was thinking about keeping her warm. She didn't tell me what she was thinking, but she kept repeating, "I don't want to wear my slacks." It was an unhappy little girl who finally trudged to school—wearing slacks under her dress.

When she returned home at noon her first words were, "I almost didn't get out to recess." Her tone was indignant and hurt. Then the real reason came out for her not wanting to wear slacks. The teacher required the children to wear during recess whatever clothes they appeared in at the beginning of the day. Although the early mornings were cool, many children dressed very lightly, and so could run out to recess with no bother. But our little girl, slow and fumbling in putting on her slacks, missed half the recess. She was embarrassed and frustrated. And all the time I thought she was just being unreasonable!

I had to face the fact that often when I've thought she was unreasonable and stubborn, there was a real reason behind the sketchy reason she offered—or failed to offer. Usually it was a fairly good one. In fact, as I surveyed our exciting and precious life with our seven-year-old, I found many reasons behind seeming unreason. I think it's worth a struggle to try to understand what lies back in the child's mind.

Finding out real reasons for puzzling behavior is often tough indeed. I phoned a number of friends with young children to ask if they had this problem. Several greeted me with the statement: "We're going through it right now!" Said one mother: "I think this is a particularly vital matter for the mother with her first child. Sometimes she is impatient, and slow to realize there is a reason behind the reason."

Why don't children, if they have a real cause for their reactions, come out with it right away? Well, oftentimes they probably don't think it through themselves. Their minds don't work like adult minds, although we parents frequently forget it. They know *how* they feel, but not always *why*. And although outwardly they seem confident, underneath they harbor lots of doubts and worries.

Being like other children seems absolutely vital to them. It is important not to be different in any way, particularly with regard to clothes. One little girl, before deciding which coat to wear to school, would keep running back and forth to her front door until she could see her best friend come out of her house across the street and find out what coat *she* was wearing. One example of what "being different" did to our daughter was that she felt humiliated because she couldn't get out to recess on time. And who has not stood at the back door time and again while the school bell rings, hearing that oft-repeated argument about leggings and boots: "No one else but me ever wears them, Mother"?

Would that all reasons behind reasons were as simple as the leggings-boots ones, harassing as these arguments become at times! How was I to guess, for instance, the reason why our little girl took a sudden aversion to wearing her new winter coat? As far as I could see, it was a perfectly good coat—blue (a color she adores), warm, becoming, and nicely sized to last for two years. But it was only after more than one tearful discussion that the real reason for our daughter's aversion appeared. Another little girl had said the coat looked like a nightgown!

A beloved T-shirt with a fat, friendly teddy bear on the front was firmly discarded by another child, who couldn't explain to his mother why. It came out eventually that someone at school had laughed at it, saying, "It's babyish."

Remarks of children can even affect more vital matters than coats and T-shirts. One small boy balked at the idea of starting kindergarten. Just when it looked as if the matter might grow serious, the child finally revealed why. A couple of his little friends had told him, "You won't know the right songs in kindergarten, because you haven't been to private nursery school like us!"

Sometimes the reason behind the reason is caused by a child's inexperience. He has had to miss school, perhaps, or church school, and doesn't want to go back. He doesn't dislike school really; he is simply afraid he can't catch up with the other children. Then he needs patient assurance on the part of both parents and teacher.

When childish fright is the reason behind the reason, it is particularly important. One day in kindergarten our little girl was late and couldn't open the door of her room. When she finally got in, she didn't want to stay. After that, if she thought she was late to school, she didn't want to go. The idea of possibly being shut out, or of meeting that whole sea of faces inside the room, was too much for her. In this case, whenever she was late, I knew why she said, "I don't want to go today." My aim had to be to get her ready in plenty of time so as to avoid this difficulty altogether.

One mother told me: "We're having a problem with our little girl because she doesn't want to walk to school alone. This morning her father stormed at her that she is spoiled. Yet, though she may be spoiled, I'm sure that's not the real reason behind this walking business." That father needs to be careful. Perhaps the child has been frightened and merely needs to face the cause of the fright, frankly and with understanding. Storming at her merely increases her fear.

Another little girl sulked and whined and would not go to

Brownie meetings because she had been elected president, a job that wasn't really very hard or important since the Brownie leader did most of the work. But that little girl didn't understand what the job entailed and it scared her.

We should remember too that sometimes the reason behind the reason that we have arguments with our children is due simply to a misunderstanding. One little boy, just graduating from tricycle age, wanted a new bicycle very badly for his birthday. Just down the street was a friend, graduating from a bike with training wheels to a big bike. So the parents of the smaller boy arranged to buy the training wheel bike for the birthday present.

Was their child happy about it? No, because this transaction was not explained to him (after all, it was to be a surprise, wasn't it?) and he didn't know his parents had paid money for the bike. He was very upset thinking that his friend was dumping on him something old that he didn't want anymore. It took a lot of explaining to bring out this reason for the child's unhappiness (in fact, he never did explain it fully; the parents had to do much guessing). But later, when he learned that providing the new training wheel bike was a loving act on the part of his parents, he could smile and appreciate the gift.

Indeed, it does take patience and understanding for us not to give up hunting for the reason behind the reason. We may well look into the areas suggested here: the desire to conform to the crowd, the desire to avoid ridicule, the uncertainties caused by inexperience and suppressed fears, or merely from an honest misunderstanding. Besides, there are many others that need to be explored. I, for one, think the search is worth it.

Any Afternoon,
Any Backyard

**It's hard to believe, but quarrels and
fights help our children grow**

One minute it was a lazy summer afternoon . . . The next
minute the stillness was rent by screams. My six-year-old
Sara, who had been playing in a neighbor's backyard, came
running, one hand on her dirty face. "Dennis—he—me—
hurt—"

When I lifted her grimy fingers from her cheek, I did see
a slight bruise.

She was still sobbing when Dennis' mother came with
Dennis in tow. "What happened?" she asked.

"I gather maybe Dennis hit her," I said.

"Did you, Dennis?" asked Dennis' mother.

Dennis, sturdy, tousle-headed, cast baleful looks at Sara.
But he set his lips grimly and said nothing.

"What happened?" I asked Sara. She was still crying and
in no mood for explaining either.

Dennis' mother and I just looked at each other.

Take any afternoon, take any backyard. Take your
backyard. Hasn't this happened to you? Because ever
since there have been children, there have been fights, and
apparently as long as there are children, there will continue to be fights.

But if it upsets you to find your own child a flailing set of
arms and legs thrashing around on the ground, or sticking his

tongue out and shouting epithets from your front lawn, take heart. A certain amount of altercation, even between friends, is part of growing up. And children learn valuable lessons thereby.

In the case of Dennis and Sara, other children reported that Dennis had been shoveling dirt into a toy wheelbarrow; Sara kept getting in his way. Whether he hit her accidentally with the shovel handle or deliberately took a whack at her, we mothers never found out. But by separating the two for the rest of the afternoon, we let them know that if they couldn't get along, play together was out. And Dennis' mother talked to him about the dangers of hitting anyone that way.

On the other hand, when there's no physical danger or damage involved, sometimes it's good to stay out of quarrels.

Once I overheard an altercation. A second-grader named Bill had found a rope. A boy named Dick was trying to get it, pulling, kicking, and shouting that it was *his!*

"It used to be," Bill panted. "But you left it in the yard. Now you only want it because I want it too!"

"That's right, Dick," spoke up another child.

"Dick, you let Bill have it," directed a slightly older child. "Finders keepers. But"—and now he was talking to Bill—"if you ever leave it around, it's finders keepers again."

But what about the fights that occur among ever-loving (or supposed to be) brothers and sisters? These are normal too.

One mother reports, "As I see the drives that motivate my children, I'm not surprised they quarrel." These are instances she recounts:

A quarrel between seven-year-old brother and little sister because she followed him while he played hide-and-seek, thus revealing his hiding place.

A quarrel between brother and his older sister who was baby-sitting him. Brother refused to take dictation from sister!

A quarrel about who would take a package to the neighbor's and thus receive the reward of a stick of chewing gum.

Actually, many brother and sister quarrels are caused by age differences which iron out later. But a major cause is the intense striving for "a place in the sun." This sense of inadequacy in the younger child lessens as he grows older. As he feels more secure about life, there isn't so much need to fight.

And authorities say that this bickering doesn't mean that our children will grow up enemies. If only once in a while they work together happily on some mutual project, we can relax. This is a good sign that basically they don't hate one another after all.

In fact, children rarely bear grudges for long. The child who was a major enemy yesterday is often the bosom friend today. Some backyard fights are just good fun too! I tried to keep this in mind when our kids "spied" on one another—a horrible practice, but one usually harmless. The same went for the fights the boys had in their homemade fort. When they threw crab apples from the tree that shaded the fort, I stayed out of it. However, when they started to throw rocks, I had to intervene.

There are some sure rules about fights, it seems to me. A child who is unfair or cruel must be reprimanded. Fighting that is dangerous or destructive must be stopped. Fights that are "grudge" fights must not be allowed. And a group that "gangs up" on some individual child should be taken to task for it.

Nevertheless, I'll grant that this continually playing Solomon on your part as a parent sometimes gets to you and you'd like to run away from it all and let someone else make the decisions. The gradation between who's right and who's wrong and whose fault was that fight or argument is very slim. And when children won't tell you what happened (and those who do tell, you have to regard as tattlers), you often feel like you're stepping off into thin air when you render a judgment. All you can do is pray a little and do your best, hoping that good intentions, based on fairness as you know it, will do the job.

There's a particular problem, of course, if it's some other child who's at fault, not your own. Mainly, it seems best to work these things through with the parents. I've never found any in our neighborhood who aren't cooperative and concerned. A little fingertip guidance on both sides can work wonders.

Actually, parents have to develop a sixth sense about fighting, anyway, to know when to intervene and when not to. If you know your own child well and the neighbors' children pretty well, it helps. Following the rules of fair play are about all you need to do. As a child grows he will learn that hitting and physical combat are out. Sharing, and sometimes giving in, are in order, along with being thoughtful of the property of others.

In the family, parents can help by treating each child alike, so that the need to fight for a place will be minimized.

Thus, fighting and quarreling during the early years seem to me to sum up this way (a parent speaking, not a psychologist!): A certain amount of fighting is normal; if it becomes habitual or if a child deliberately "picks" fights, then it requires special concern.

One day when our little girl was playing with three neighborhood children, they couldn't decide what to do. Two wanted to "dress up"; another, to play a quiet game inside; and the other one wanted to go outdoors. Finally they got to arguing. When they were about to come to blows, I suggested they draw straws.

The straws decreed they play outdoors. But the girl who wanted to play a quiet game indoors had a hard time giving in. "Don't sulk," the others said. "This is the fair way."

Still, from her expression I could see the battle she was having. But when the others left, she stood there only a moment alone. Then, with a purposeful look, she went to join them.

That girl had made a little progress in growing up that

morning. There had been learning in the quarrel and profit from it. Thus can quarrels and fights help our children to grow. And before we know it, our backyards and houses will be calm and still. Our children won't be playing there as before. Instead, they'll be grown up.

III

As Parents–
We Worship
God

The end of learning is to know God.
John Milton

Church Away from Home

There is something about public worship —even while on vacation—that a family can't get anywhere else

I remember that conversation well, even now. Our family was staying at a cottage on the lake. We had just finished a leisurely breakfast and were sitting around trying to decide what to do next—go fishing, boating, or just lie around in the sun.

"It's such a glorious Sunday morning," remarked my husband, "we ought to do something special."

"Sunday? It's Sunday?" Our young son, who was just learning the days of the week, spoke up. He frowned, trying to figure it out. "Aren't we going to Sunday school?"

"Oh, it's vacation—" I began, and stopped.

Our ten-year-old daughter joined in. "Oops! I almost forgot. I *have* to go to Sunday school. If I don't, I'll break my attendance record."

So on that particular vacation Sunday, an attendance record was the reason we went to church.

It was a small resort town with only one Protestant church —not far from the business district on the main street of the one-street village. There we saw a simple white frame structure with a square, sturdy bell tower. The building was shared by two denominations. The first held services at an early hour, the second at ten and eleven. Since we were already too late for the first service, ten o'clock found our older daughter in a church school class with her age-group.

I accompanied our little boy to his age-group while Dad took care of our toddler.

At eleven o'clock all of us were in the sanctuary together for church.

When the services were dismissed, many people came up and spoke to us. "I suppose you have a lot of visitors," I remarked, thinking how large the lake area was and how many vacationers' cottages dotted the shore.

The local church member shook her head. "Not too many," she admitted. She went on frankly, "Really not many at all."

Her words echoed in my ears. I kept going back to my own words earlier that morning when our little boy had suggested going to Sunday school. I hadn't meant my reply to sound the way it did when I'd said, "Oh, it's vacation—"

Vacation? Vacation from what? God? Worship? Prayer?

Later when my husband and I were talking it over, I said flatly: "Well, we have to face it. Families don't do very well at going to church away from home."

"Is there any reason why this particular family couldn't do better?" suggested my husband.

Thus a wonderful experience started for us. We decided then and there that Sunday was for church school and church, wherever we might be.

"Isn't it hard sometimes," a friend remarked one day, "when you're busy traveling? Suppose you want to be on the road early for a long day's trip."

"No, it's not hard," I told her, and I meant it. "Not when we put church into our Sunday plans ahead of time. Besides, we have found that many churches hold early morning services, particularly in the summer months."

"Look," said another, "I find all the inspiration I need out on the lake, watching the sunrise when I'm fishing or just gazing off into the hills."

"True," I said, "God is near when you look at a sunrise, or at the wonders of nature. But we feel there is something about going into his house that you can't get anywhere else.

And somehow there are always a lot of distractions when you are outdoors—a fish may bite your line or a mosquito may bite you. Where do your meditations go then?"

"But don't your children get tired of it?" suggested someone else.

"That's the beautiful part of it," I was able to say truthfully. "They're even more eager to go than we are. And my husband and I feel it pretty important that they learn now that Sunday is, in a special way, God's day; that no matter where we are, we go to his house to worship him. Else how can we expect them to make the effort to go when they are older, remembering that Mother and Dad only went when they had nothing else to do?"

Well, that is the story of that one summer, and how we started going to church when away from home. But the story does not end there. Once we started, we kept it up, even though the attendance record which initiated it was now a thing of the past.

"I guess we just keep going because we like it," someone remarked.

Why did I like it? I tried to sort it out. "Like" was perhaps not the correct word. What meaning was this experience having for me? It was interesting to notice the development of my thinking about it.

I had long thought of vacation with its relaxed program—its lazy, restful moments in the sun—as a time to reexamine goals, to ask God to redirect my life for another year. How much better it was to begin each week of this period in a house of worship with others who were also seeking the assurance of God's strength and guidance.

Speaking for myself, I can think of several other reasons why I feel it is important to go to church when away from home. I like to start each new week by going to church—reviewing mistakes of the past week, asking God for guidance for the next one. This, I feel, is just as vital when I'm away from home as when I'm at home. And my week always seems to go better, begun this way.

And there is value in visiting other churches. We have attended services of other denominations when we were unable to find our own. It's been interesting to compare these services with those of our church. In this way different denominations have become more than just names as a true ecumenical spirit develops.

Besides all this, there is always the inspiration of the sermon. We have heard many fine ministers. One sermon in particular proved so helpful that I made notes and still refer to them.

As for church school, I have found it fascinating and instructive to read different lesson materials and to observe how they are taught. As a church school teacher, I sometimes have accompanied one of my children to the class in order to listen and learn.

We have found others always cooperative and respectful of our churchgoing. When we go off to church while visiting, usually our hosts rout themselves out and go with us.

Nowadays there is much emphasis on things families can do together. It seems to me that at the top of this list should be going to church together. One of the dearest memories of my childhood is going to church with my mother and father. Now that we have our own family, it's always been a thrill when visiting my hometown to attend this church where I was baptized and where the children's dad and I were married. When we've visited my husband's parents we've found that the most accessible church is of another denomination than ours. Their church school is held after the main church service, an interesting new experience.

Going to church away from home is simple once you try it. There is time for it, there is inspiration and education in it, there is a wonderful example for children in it. Best of all, there is God in it.

Sometimes I think of the five of us as the total of church visitors in that little resort town on that first summer weekend. Why don't more of us attend church school and church away from home? No vacation trip is complete without it.

Grace
at Our House

Saying grace before meals starts a habit children will not soon forget

It sometimes happened when we were in a hurry. Dad, rushing in from work, would sit down to lunch with an "I don't have much time" look on his face.

Here's the picture: Seven-year-old Bruce tore in, shouting, "I want to get back to play in the school yard before the bell rings!" Twelve-year-old Jane entered in a more leisurely fashion but immediately said, "I hope lunch is ready, because I have a date to meet some of the girls." Hearing all this, Sara, the youngest, clambered into her chair while Mother hastened to put food on the table. As we sat down, at least one person was likely to begin to eat without waiting.

But then someone always remembered. Often it was Sara or Bruce, or it might be one of the adults. "Stop! We forgot to say grace." So down went knives and forks, and five heads bowed for a short period of thanksgiving before resuming lunch and family chatter.

Usually, of course, we all wait for grace as we first start a meal. But the heartening thing about the hurried times when we might overlook it is that the children never let us! Grace had been a part of their lives for as long as they could remember. Mealtime did not seem complete to them without it.

Prayer at mealtime became a family business for us easily and naturally. In my childhood home my father returned thanks. But I too had a child's grace, written by my mother, and at times I was asked to say it at our table.

Upon our marriage, my husband and I agreed we would continue grace-giving, but since his preferred method is silent grace, we would take turns. And, unexpectedly, taking turns continued as the pattern in our much larger family picture, because who should want to take turns with us next but our first daughter, when she was three years old? She was followed by our son and then by our younger daughter, all of them begging to have turns.

What should they say?

The pattern had already been set for this too. My husband and I had our own graces; so why shouldn't each of the children have his or her own?

I'll admit that older sister Jane's prayer is a little informal. Cherishing my mother's original grace, I thought I would write one for my daughter too. But one day when she was clamoring loudly at mealtime for "something to say" and would not be put off until my poetic mood could be set to work, I hastily improvised a few sentences for her. They continued over the years and were used by little sister Sara as her grace too.

Not to be caught unprepared again, I searched through printed graces. Together Bruce and I selected the one he liked best.

It goes like this:

> Thank you for the food we eat;
> Thank you for the friends we meet;
> Thank you for our work and play;
> Thank you, God, for a happy day.
>   (Jennie Lou Milton)

Older sister Jane's words that we thought up on the spur of the moment are: "Thank thee, God, for this food. Watch over and keep us. Amen."

My own grace, written by my mother, reads:

Our Father, we thank thee for giving us food;
    We ask thy blessing today;
We thank thee for clothing and all things good,
    And for the needy we pray.
Our Father, we ask thee to help us today
    To do the things that we should.
To smile and scatter along the way
    The joy that comes from doing good.

Of course silent grace poses no problem and makes a nice variation in the pattern of thanksgiving. And for those who have the inclination, I think my father's type of grace, the real old-fashioned extemporaneous kind, given in rich, rolling tones, is one of the most inspiring memories a child can have.

But a friend of mine insists that though she feels sorry that they do not have grace in their home, it always seems stilted to her. "I feel self-conscious about it," she says.

I have already suggested how to avoid this. Feel natural about it yourself, and let the children participate!

Another picture: True, when Bruce offered his prayer, he was apt to mumble and go too fast. Sara often had to be prompted. Occasionally, Jane needed help in creating a new prayer. In silent grace they also sometimes, beneath lowered eyes, sampled a tiny first bite of food before time was up. As for my more formal grace, it hasn't been often used except on Sundays. But even though the moment is not always perfect, it's definitely worth it.

In a more general sense it's interesting that the word "blessing" is used interchangeably with "grace." This word can be interpreted in several ways. Isn't it a blessing when we take time to stop and think of God before meals? In addition, we are thanking God for his blessings—his diverse gifts in life —when we use a grace such as Bruce chose with all the "thank you's" in it. And we ask God's blessings on these same gifts to us as expressed in the type of grace used by some close friends of ours:

Come, Lord Jesus,
Be our guest.
Let these gifts
To us be blest.

Most of us think of grace as being part of mealtime at
home. But on occasion people pause to say grace in restau-
rants. Sometimes a family will fold hands and bow heads at
one table among the many, amid the chatter of voices and
clatter of dishes. Subsequently a sort of hush can be noticed
among those who are sitting nearby who realize that grace
is being said. What a way for that family to witness!

Some families also join hands around the table during
grace. One husband and wife I know each lay a hand on the
table and his hand goes over hers, or hers over his, as they
quietly touch and share the blessing.

Why do we believe in grace at our house? For many reasons. Partly it is because we know that to snatch moments
for family worship and thanksgiving in this busy world is
difficult, and the habit needs cultivation. Partly it is because
my husband and I want our children to grow up knowing
that God cares for them and is always near. They can talk
to him at any time. Finally, we want them to know that there
is a something in life bigger and more important than material things.

Actually, we haven't talked much to our children about
these goals. We have just told them that God has been good
to us and that we want to thank him. By our keeping it
simple, they have accepted grace as an integral part of our
home life.

Then, when they establish their own homes, we hope the
habit of saying grace will come full circle for our children.
Here is the picture: Not our child, but a young grandchild,
reminding the dinner table where hurried parents and perhaps
a brother or sister are seated: "You forgot to say grace." So
down will go knives and forks, and heads will bow for a short
period of thanksgiving to the One to whom we owe so much.

Keeping
God Real

God is very real to children. It's up to us parents to help them not to lose that special, intimate feeling

Children have a wonderful concept of God. Watching our two youngest, Bruce and Sara, impressed upon me how close they feel toward him and how real he is to them—as real as their mother and father and playmates on the street. Yet I find that many of us grown-ups have lost this closeness. God has ceased to be a person to us. When we adults set the children such a poor example, it is easy to see why they lose their sense of nearness to God. I've been wondering what we, as parents, can do to preserve that trust and faith so natural in the young.

How do young children look at God? Bruce's ideas are a sample. Once when he was small he wanted me to clear up the point as to whether God was a man or a woman. He believed that God was up in the sky and told me one day that we'd have to yell loud if we wanted to make God hear! Throwing a ball into the air, he wondered what would happen if God "ketched" the ball and threw it back down. God is real and concrete.

Children accept literally the fact of God's power to create. My son once made the comment that "if God made eyeballs for people, he must have a lot of things up there." He questioned God's having made "skeeters," however, since so many people don't like mosquitoes! On the other hand, my daughter Sara chided me because I had said there could be no thunder and lightning in winter—and then there *was* a thunderstorm in January! "God can do anything he wants to, can't he?" she remarked. "Then let him!"

Children believe that God takes notice of what they are doing. Maybe my son had God mixed up with parents when he remarked that God doesn't like children to say "no"—but he credited the thought to God, nevertheless. And Sara remarked to me as the baby next door was crying, "Don't you wish you were God so you'd know what the baby is crying about?"

True, adulthood brings a more realistic point of view and clears up some of the magic that is part of a child's world. But there is nothing basically wrong with the child's complete trust. Did not Jesus say, "Verily I say unto you, Except ye . . . become as little children, ye shall not enter into the kingdom of heaven" (Matt. 18:3, KJV) ?

How, then, does God become only someone to pray to formally at night and to think about on Sunday? Why?

I've begun to ponder about the example my husband and I set in our home in our attitude toward God. True, we have grace at meals, and I've taught the children to say good-night prayers. The children go to Sunday church school, and my husband and I are members of the church. I could rate us as average Christians. But what about our personal relationship with God? As our children grow, what can we parents do to help them keep that sense of God's power and presence, so real to them in their early childhood?

First, we can bring out in the open some of our own thoughts about God as a friend. If our children know we feel God close to us, that we call upon him often to help us, they are likely to do the same.

When our daughter Sara was ill, we talked about the new "wonder drugs" and how thankful we were for what they did for her. We were profuse, too, in our praise of the doctor's unflagging efforts. But what about God? Did he have any part in Sara's recovery?

As is true with most of us, fear made me break through the thick fog of neglect between myself and a God I had been taking for granted. Actually, I prayed in private, earnestly and long, but the children didn't know it. I believe they *should* know about the strength that comes to me from calling on God in times of distress.

We can encourage our children to talk to God at any time, day or night. One day when the way opened, I said to my daughter, "When I'm bone-tired, during one of those days when nothing goes right, I often ask God to give me strength to just get through until night. You'd be surprised how much better I feel!"

Sara was thoughtful. Presently she said, "Tomorrow at school I have to give a report." She shivered a little. "I always get scared. Do you think if I asked God to help me not to be afraid, it would work?"

"Of course it would!" I assured her.

"It's wonderful, isn't it," she remarked finally, "to know that God is with us wherever we are, wanting to help us!"

Later she came to me to talk over some other school matters. With my new resolve in mind, I suggested: "First, let's ask God to help in your decision. Then we can know that whatever course we take is the right one."

Then my son had his hamster out on the front step playing with it and it got away. He wanted to pray that God would bring it back, but he wanted to look for it too.

"I'm glad you feel that way," I told him. "We will look for the hamster and you can ask your boyfriends and their parents to keep a watch out for it. Always we have to do our best. Then we can ask God to take over."

When the hamster wasn't found, I was afraid my son might feel that God had let him down. But I want my children to know that there is more to praying than just asking for something, that prayer must include, "Thy will be done."

We can share with our children our certainty that we need not fear, because God will be with us, no matter what happens.

Ours is a world of fear. Recently a man in our small community met death in mysterious and frightening circumstances. My older daughter came home from school with the tale, upset and worried. When I admonished her not to be afraid, she countered with, "How can I help but be?" Then, turning to the morning paper, she read aloud the front-page headlines. What a grisly lot they were!—war, death and destruction, tax scandals, bad accidents, and gangland shootings.

But in spite of the horrible things that are happening and undoubtedly will still happen, I believe that my children need not be afraid. The only way I know to put away fear is through faith in God and a belief in God's purposes. Specifically, I can teach my children familiarity with Bible verses, such as, "I sought the Lord, and he heard me, and delivered me from all my fears" (Ps. 34:4, KJV). Or I can help them say in their own words, simply and sincerely, "God is with me. I need not be afraid."

We can go to church more often as a family. We can encourage participation in church youth groups, in the Sunday church school, in church projects. I feel that when children are at last on their own, association with the church will help to keep them close to God.

Yes, I mean to rededicate myself to keeping God real to my children. As I try, I know that other ways will be opened to us. It shouldn't be hard, because he is so real to them already.

When Bruce was younger, he sometimes expressed his annoyance with his little sister in terms of his very personal relationship to God. One day when Sara was banging noisily on a pan lid, he remarked plaintively: "Make her stop, Mother! I can't even hear God!"

I, as a grown-up, am afraid that too often in the past I couldn't hear God. But as a parent I'm going to start over again. For, in spite of my forgetfulness, I know that God is always near enough to be heard, if I but listen, sure of his reality, his closeness. There is no more important knowledge to share with my children.

Seeing
Stars

Studying the stars in an uncertain world can help to bolster a belief that God is still in charge

Flashing lights on airplanes! UFOs! Astronauts! The sky is full of objects these nights. We grown-ups crane our necks to look at what is up there, and so do the youngsters. What do we see? Amid the whirling man-made phenomena, we also see the stars.

But there is more to it than this. After that first glance, our family looked again and again. Take it from us, a continued interest in "seeing stars" can be a lot of fun. We found that star study does not cost anything, can be done almost anywhere, and has no age limits. Also, it is as old as time and as new as tomorrow. For our part, we started out to identify constellations, but we were led on and on, culminating in a particular interest in searching out religious references to the stars.

It all started when we went to visit our children's grandparents one summer. There, in the stillness of an Indiana farm night, the sky was dark. Over the barn hung the constellation of the Big Dipper. As a star enthusiast from way back, I was delighted with this opportunity to share my constellation knowledge with the children, particularly with our ten-year-old son, Bruce, avidly interested in everything around him.

It was enough at first to locate the pointers of the Big

Dipper, which lead to Polaris, the North Star, long a guide for navigators. Then we tried to make out the outline of the bowl and the handle of the dipper.

One thing led to another. The next day we went to town and bought a star guide. That night, sky charts in hand, we stood in the farmyard, studying star locations, while flipping our older daughter's Girl Scout flashlight on and off as first we'd look at the book, then at the sky.

The constellations that do not "set" at our latitude (40 degrees), the circumpolar ones, so called, were the first we sought out, moving from the Big Dipper to the Little Dipper, which has the North or Pole Star at the end of its handle, then to Draco the dragon, to Cepheus the king, and finally to Cassiopeia the queen, seated in a chair, which has the shape of a W. What if it does take imagination to visualize these figures? Imagination is what youngsters have in abundance. Mine accepted with alacrity the explanation that constellations are pictures made up by man as a handy way to map the sky, and that most of the characters and objects used come from Greek or Roman mythology.

In the meantime I had sneaked in a little extra reading. So I asked the youngsters to guess how many stars they were seeing that night, a clear and velvety one, with the Milky Way brilliantly displayed. The guesses ranged from a million (our seven-year-old), to ten thousand (our ten-year-old), to two thousand (our Girl Scout). The last number was about right, but practically unbelievable at that, since there are thousands more stars visible only by telescope, still more to be seen only in other seasons of the year, and still others in the southern hemisphere which we never see!

It was practically unbelievable, too, to realize how far away the sun is, which is our closest star. At 93 million miles from the earth, it is almost 300,000 times closer than the next star, which is 26 million million miles away. Translating this into light-years, each of which represents the distance that light travels in one year—it moves at about 186,281 miles per second—is not much better: the closest star, except the sun, is still about 4.4 light-years away.

If this wasn't enough to cut us down to size, another fact was: Stars shine by their own light. Much of the light that was reaching the earth that night had left the most distant stars long before there were civilized people on earth—or in some cases before there were people on earth at all!

We also talked about the fact that astronomy is the oldest of the sciences, and this brought us to our first Biblical reference. Some ancient lore credits Noah as being one of the earliest astronomers. This caused Bruce to ask, "Then did these same stars shine on Abraham and Moses?" I was able to tell him yes, they had.

Later that summer we went on vacation in Wisconsin. It was Bruce's idea to go out in a boat for a better view of the stars. It turned out to be a good one. As we rowed out beyond the tree line, the whole sky rose above us, star-studded. Putting the oars aside, letting the boat drift, we sat and drank it all in, passing back and forth the binoculars Bruce had received for Christmas. They were 8-power, for bird-watching, but strong enough to bring within vision many fainter stars.

Then, carefully lowering himself from his seat, Bruce found the best way of all to observe the stars—lying on his back in the bottom of the boat. Above his head was the Northern Cross, with the bright star, Deneb, at its top, and on one side the brightest summer star of all, Vega in Lyra the lyre, and on the other, Altair in Aquila the eagle.

As I pointed out the cross to Bruce, he asked immediately, having absorbed the idea that all constellations have some extra meaning, "Is that Jesus' cross?"

I'd read up on that, too, since once I became interested in the Biblical background of star lore, I devoured several books that our minister had borrowed from a theological seminary library. I told Bruce that the real mythological significance of the constellation made it Cygnus the swan, but that, "yes, early Christians had connected the constellation with the cross on which Christ was crucified." I also mentioned that Draco the dragon, a long and twisting constellation, was designated at one time as a snake, perhaps the snake in the Garden of Eden, or the crooked serpent in Job 26:13 (KJV).

This brought us back to the Big Dipper, which, when extended to include other nearby stars, is also known as Ursa Major, or the Great Bear, just as the Little Dipper is known as Ursa Minor, or the Little Bear. In the Middle Ages, Ursa Major was regarded by some as one of the bears sent by the prophet Elisha to "punish his juvenile persecutors."

In the autumn, back home, when the constellation Orion finally became visible over the horizon, Bruce and I talked more about all of this. He was especially interested to learn that the stars serve three ways to give actual guidance: to tell time, direction, and position.

After watching the brilliant stars in Orion the hunter, and then viewing nearby the small cluster of the Pleiades, the seven sisters, we went inside the house and opened the Bible, the Revised Standard Version. There, in Job 9:9, Bruce read, "[God] made the Bear and Orion, the Pleiades and the chambers of the south."

This is not the only place in Job where constellations are mentioned. Job 38:31 speaks of the Pleiades and Orion again; in v. 32 the writer speaks of the Bear and Mazzaroth, or the twelve signs, suggested as the belt of twelve constellations in the Zodiac, or the "chambers" through which the sun seems to pass successively in the course of a year, its "resting place" for a month.

On the other hand, as we read the King James Version of the Bible, in Job 38:32 we discovered, instead of the Bear, the name of Arcturus, one of the brightest stars, which appears in the constellation Boötes the herdsman and is on a line with the handle of the Big Dipper.

Others than Job speak of stars in the Old Testament. In Amos 5:8 (RSV) both the Pleiades and Orion are mentioned. Reference in Isaiah 13:10 to "constellations" may mean

Orion, termed by some "the most splendid constellation in the sky."

Carrying the phraseology further, we believe our family interest in Orion and his starry friends, "the most splendid" interest imaginable. Besides this, I believe that our "seeing stars," which has extended far beyond that one summer, has had another, more important benefit: I feel that the stars, in their quiet predictability, can become a point of reference. Bret Harte called them "patient stars." Justice Oliver Wendell Holmes had this to say: "These stars in their courses, where they have been for aeons of time, are the real symbol of the meaning of our times. God is in control of his universe."

In these days of uncertainty, our youngsters certainly need to develop the feeling that God is in control. It is hoped, among other uses, that "seeing stars" can help build this concept into young lives.

Why Not
Hymns at Home?

**If the sound of music at home is the
sound of hymn-singing, it can be rewarding
indeed**

Surprising as it may seem, the most popular music book on
our piano is a hymnal. Not because anyone set up a campaign
to make it popular. Its appearance on the piano and its
subsequent frequent usage came about by accident. Now that
it has become so well liked, it is no accident that it will stay
on the piano. After all, our family has learned the joy of
singing hymns at home.

By chance I was the catalyst in bringing this happy situation about. A longtime church school teacher, I also doubled
as accompanist when needed. "Needed" in this instance because of the illness of the regular pianist, I found I could do
with some practicing of the hymns I was expected to play.
So I carried the hymnal home with me and, when I had a
minute, sat down at the piano and went over the songs we
were currently using in our church school primary depart-
ment.

A particularly good time for practicing turned out to be
following dinner after my jobs for the day were about
finished. And since the piano is in the living room and the
television in the family room, I wasn't interfering with anyone. But I had no sooner started one night when Sara, our
five-year-old, turned up.

"I like that song," she said. "What is it?"

"It's called 'I Love to Tell the Story,' " I explained. "It does have a nice tune. But it's fairly long. It might be too old for you."

"It's not," she replied staunchly (at this point this was her constant response about age, with the hope that we'd believe she could *always* keep up with any of us).

This time she was right. While the verses were rather long, the refrain (chorus) was short and suitable and easy to learn. Presently she and I were singing the whole song together and enjoying it.

Since Sara is our family "songbird" anyway, at the time I didn't think much about this interest of hers and just kept thumping along with my practice, because the regular pianist remained ill for several weeks. More and more often, Sara joined me. Then older sister Jane, a thirteen-year-old high schooler, caught the fever. Sitting down at the piano to play some of the popular music she had begun to acquire, she'd try the hymnbook first. Turning a few pages to find a hymn she was familiar with, she'd play it and then perhaps go on to others. Sometimes she never even got to her popular music because of preoccupation with the hymnal.

That left only Bruce, our eight-year-old, uninvolved. What finally caught him was one of the livelier hymns. When he wandered into the living room one evening I purposely started to sing the opening line of the hymn I was practicing: "Truehearted, wholehearted, faithful and loyal"—words that had begun to have some meaning for him. He wandered nearer and peered over my shoulder, trying to read the verse himself with his newly acquired third-grade skills.

He didn't stay long that night but I could see he liked the phraseology of the refrain to that one: "Peal out the watchword! Silence it never!" Presently he too made it a duet when this hymn was played.

Well, well, I thought. How contemporary the hymns actually are.

I really hadn't studied a hymnal previously. There had been other ones on our family music shelf before this particu-

lar one took its place on our piano. Those other hymnals were
old. One or two had belonged to my mother and one had been
my grandmother's. As I opened carefully the faded, thumb-
marked covers and turned the now brittle and browning
pages, the one thing that impressed me was how well worn
these books were—obviously used and loved. And I remembered my grandmother telling me that, as a very young girl
when she went away from home for the first time to teach
school, it seemed a tremendous, even scary step into an un-
known world—in those days without quick communications
and travel. So as she was departing, she asked her mother and
brother to join her in singing "The Unclouded Day," a hymn
their family loved, in order to bolster her courage.

Courage from hymns? Why not? I thought of some of the
hymns about Jesus I was playing. "What a Friend We Have
in Jesus." If that doesn't bolster you, what does? I found
other hymns that can be helpful in building lives. How about
"I Would Be True" and "Give of Your Best to the Master"?
Don't these extol characteristics we all hope to develop and
to carry over from our spiritual lives into our temporal ones?

This could be one reason I noticed that the hymnal on our
piano had no trouble competing with the other music already
there—Sara's nursery and kindergarten songs, Bruce's cowboy songs, and Jane's popular ones. I even noticed that when
Jane's girl friends were calling for her they would drop down
at the piano while they waited and, more often than not, the
hymnal caught their attention too.

Then the hymnal began to vanish for a few days at a time
as Diane, Jane's friend across the street, began borrowing it.
That was the signal for me to do something about it. So I
arranged to buy copies for our family and Diane. Now it was
our own hymnal we were using. Now there was no reason to
think that hymns relate only to church school and Sundays.
They're for every day in the week.

I began to analyze the hymns our children liked best.
Mostly they were the ones they had learned already in church
school. They liked the specially rhythmic ones: "I Want to

Be a Christian" and "Stand Up, Stand Up for Jesus." The specially melodic ones: "I Love to Tell the Story," "Fairest Lord Jesus," and "I Think When I Read That Sweet Story of Old." And the specially thankful ones: "For the Beauty of the Earth" and "This Is My Father's World."

Occasionally some nights I even managed to get the whole family together, including Dad, to sing "Now the Day Is Over." We two parents felt particularly touched as we watched the children disperse to their rooms to study or to go to bed, still humming that beautiful tune.

Christmas carols? They are good to review any season of the year. Since, like many mothers, I am concerned how to make Christmas a less commercial and more deeply reverent celebration, I know of no finer way to approach this than through song.

It may sound from all this as though we are an extraordinarily musical family. Such is not the case. In some ways I'd say we are a little submusical, though I play the piano and Jane had the usual quota of piano lessons. But I have no doubt at all that any average family would succumb to the appeal of hymns-made-available as we have.

The fact is that hymns are likable and tremendously singable. They stand on their own and can meet the stiffest musical competition if given a chance. I've decided that it's up to us as parents to make them available to our children, without any fanfare or lectures as to their value. The children will find this out for themselves—as our own children did. And that is what we want them to do!

Your Child
and Death

An honest explanation of death will help the child get on normally with living

Nearly all families will suffer at least one death as a child is growing up.

Often parents attempt to soften the idea of death by some fairy tale. One adult relates that as a child she was told that a friend died because God loved her so much he wanted to take her to him. Later, she was afraid of God, afraid he would love her so much he would cause her to die, too.

Children, told that death is like sleep, sometimes become afraid of bedtime and falling asleep. Told that "only the old die," a child may be afraid of growing up and becoming old.

A parent would do well to think ahead of time what to say to a child about death, so as not to have to grab out of the air some tale remembered from childhood. If, to shield a child, a parent does not talk about death, the child may interpret this to mean that the adult is frightened, and if so, where can a child turn? Indeed, what he imagines can be far worse than the truth about death.

Of course, the same explanations about death cannot be made to all children. There are differences in temperament; some youngsters are more excitable than others. However, most differences in approach come because of the age of the child.

Studies show that the concept children have about death

is not nearly as gruesome as people imagine. From ages three to five a child will think of death as reversible. In the "Bang, bang, you're dead" game everyone gets up. When Daddy goes away to the office he always comes back. From ages five to nine a child knows that others die but doesn't realize he or she will someday die. It is only at age nine to ten that acceptance comes of eventual death.

Some people think that if a young child seems not to care or shows little grief at a death in the family, he is not feeling it. This is not true. If a child seems not to be deeply affected, it may be because he is pretending death has not occurred, that the person is still alive. Because the loss is too great for him to accept, he hides his feelings of grief, even from himself.

Some helps for parents wanting to know how to approach the subject of death with their children are these:

• First, and probably most important, is to encourage a child to "talk out" his questions and feelings about death. To put fear into words often exorcises it or at least puts it into perspective. Talking also allows a parent to correct misconceptions.

• Using everyday experiences when explaining about death may be helpful. Children at nearly all ages know what a cemetery is and have seen dead birds, fish, or dogs.

• For the early ages a simple unemotional explanation may suffice: Death occurs when the body wears out or sometimes is the result of an accident.

Taking a child to a funeral is another way to help him accept death's reality. (But a child should not be taken if he resists the idea.)

• A younger child may need to be reassured that he is in no danger of dying himself, that his parents are not going to die, or if one has died, that he will still be taken care of.

From this it can be seen that the young child, roughly through the elementary years, views death quite personally with the thought of *what will happen to me?* The high schooler is not likely to react the same way. He has a greater backlog of experience to rely on, likewise he does not feel so weak and dependent. But he has also the disadvantage of trying to think things through to a greater extent. He is usually endeavoring to sort out his ideas about God, heaven, and the soul, perhaps with some worry and uncertainty.

It is hoped that the parent will have accepted death as a part of life, feeling it neither terrifying nor dreadful; this will enable him to impart to his offspring his own comforting philosophy.

Parents would do well to remember what one minister points out—that the tragedy of death inevitably tempts us to despair or prompts us to faith. Blessed is the child whose parents' deep-seated faith witnesses to the belief that God is with us in our darkest moments, that he suffers with us, and that our pain is his pain. Such faith not only conquers parental fears but a child's as well.

Nevertheless, no one can state, *"This* is what you should say, not *that,"* for it is a highly individual and personal matter. A parent should not feel embarrassed to call on the minister to help out here if needed. Certainly, in a church-related family, the minister is the first person likely to come to the house at the time of death. For puzzled and shaken teen-agers, the minister's explanation of a calm, certain faith can be most helpful.

Added to the responsibility of telling children about death and helping them to accept it, parents have another function. This is to aid children to work through their grief.

"Keeping busy" is an important facet here. In order to give children stability, it is vital to keep family life moving along, even in the days before a funeral. Children should be given the opportunity to feel useful and needed in this family crisis. Teen-agers are old enough to do many errands, assist in a small way with decisions. Younger children can help around the house, answering the door or phone.

As the weeks wear on, keeping busy still retains importance. Many family members have become closer-knit because of a death, developing deeper love in the family circle than ever before.

It is also important to continue to talk freely about the one who has died, citing his good points and the good times had with him. A home where a lost parent or child is still warmly remembered in conversation has taken a long step toward assuaging grief.

Such memories should also be shared freely with old friends and neighbors, whose concern and care will help grieving children and young people adjust to their loss better.

Mourning has several stages. First, there is protest against the death, accompanied by anxiety, yearning, preoccupation with the dead person, and perhaps by anger and guilt. Next there are pain, despair, disorganization, which marks the beginning of acceptance. Finally, there is hope, as new goals and new people enter into life and activities once more take on meaning. Indeed, this progression of grief is valuable and necessary to the process of healing.

While the preceding description of grief presumably applies to an adult, it can also be applied to a child.

Children will gain confidence and strength if they are not shielded unduly from the facts of death, if their parents are open and honest in their explanations, if they truly sympathize, and if their own faith in God's purposes is strong. Then the children will, in turn, be able to face the facts of death, express their own feelings and fears about it, and be comforted and reassured. Only then, with new hope, can they get on normally with the business of living.

When We Worship at Home

Informal worship is one way we can witness our beliefs to our children

It was a Sunday afternoon in early summer. Seven-year-old Bruce ran into the house from outdoor play. He tugged at my hand. He beckoned to his father. "Come out, come out. We're going to have church."

When we followed him, we found he had in fact planned "church." He had brought a Bible from inside the house, he had made a sort of altar with a chair, and he had put pillows on the grass for us to sit on. With us and his younger sister looking on, he then proceeded to conduct "worship." Even though his remarks were a little garbled, it was very moving.

Indeed, this showed us that ages six to eight, roughly the first three grades in school, are the rich years for sharing family worship with children. The child in this age range is rather literal about religion.

Sara, at six, wanted to send Jesus a Christmas card. Bruce, of a more scientific bent, considered how God lights the sky "up there" and all over the world. With this type of interest, these children do not have to be coerced or disciplined to participate in family worship.

Two times of day seem natural for worship—mealtime and bedtime.

When I was growing up, my family read from the Gospels each morning at breakfast. Other families—either morning

or evening—have a more extended service, including besides
Bible reading, prayers and songs.

Then there is grace before meals, sometimes with all at the
table joining hands.

Bedtime is story time for most young children. In Christian homes children also say their prayers. For family worship this can be expanded. Sometimes the whole family can
gather at the youngest child's bedside, discussing the day's
happenings and problems, also each giving thanks for what
was good about the day.

Music can also be used. Bruce had a record player in his
room. Playing "The Lord's Prayer" on it became a regular
feature of bedtime, and Sara, hearing it from her room, would
join him in singing.

At this early age there are also opportunities for spontane-
ous worship, such as Bruce presented in his outdoor church.
When Sara came into the kitchen and wanted me to sing
"Onward, Christian Soldiers" with her at the piano, it would
have been foolish to say, "Wait until I finish the dishes." I
knew that by then her mood might have changed. So I dried
my hands and went—right then.

There have been many other such unplanned moments of
worship in our family, often in connection with the beauties
of nature—a quick prayer of gratitude in the car after viewing
the Grand Canyon, reverent quiet as we all stood viewing an
unexpected rainbow.

Special seasons of the year lend themselves to special worship programs. Christmas Eve *en famille* is a particularly
precious time. It is often wise to rely upon an outside source
for a service for this. We used one our church school pre-
pared. As in a play, there were parts for each child and for
us parents and the hymns "O Little Town of Bethlehem" and
"Away in a Manger" to be sung.

New Year's, Easter, July 4, Thanksgiving, Christmas—the
list of seasonal events is long if families want to plan a special
worship service for each of them.

It is amazing how many different forms of family worship

there can be. An informal period of family talk, threshing out problems, telling happenings from school, recounting the lesson from church school, even discussing episodes from television can be worship-related and Christian-oriented.

Such a flexible and varied approach can help overcome several so-called obstacles to family worship today. One is the feeling that such worship has to follow certain prescribed patterns.

To get away from this, why not take as the definition of family worship: focusing attention on God, not ourselves? Under this credo it is possible to view informal worship tailored to a family's personal needs as exactly right.

The argument that there cannot be family worship today because there is not enough time does not hold up before a plan of flexible worship. Certainly some shared moments can be squeezed in somewhere.

That is not to say that families should not try for more formal, extensive worship sessions at a certain time daily or once a week.

But here we come to a third hazard. This is the feeling that worship has to be deeply inspirational each time it occurs. It won't be. Some days people's moods just won't fit in; prayers will seem wooden. The children, normally so responsive, will be engrossed in something else—perhaps a magic show they are getting up or a program at school.

But it won't be forever. And maybe discouragement has its uses. After a few days of despair about family worship, we are moved to try harder.

If there is one thing the little child loves, it is to play grown-up. When interest waned with Bruce, we suggested that *he* help plan the service. This led us to the Bible for a suitable story, a selection of songs that *he* found meaningful.

To sustain interest further, we varied reading from the Bible with reading well-illustrated Bible stories, and switched from the King James Version to some of the modern versions, supplemented at times with books of devotions. We also gave time to discussing Bible passages or the words of

a song. And we made opportunities for the children to participate.

As soon as Bruce could read, he read aloud from his own
Bible. Sara started and stopped the record player or turned
pages for me when I played the piano; later, she was able to
read, too.

Stressing the concept of "talking to God," we encouraged
the children to make up their own prayers. Their father and
I tried to see that our adult ones were not too abstract. When
a friend of the children was ill, we prayed for him; when
Bruce had a new teacher, we prayed for her. We talked about
what there was to be thankful for—at home, on our street,
at school—and gave thanks for these things.

Undoubtedly children of this age do not understand the
deeper implications of worship, yet—with their free, unfet-
tered approach to life—perhaps they understand it better
than we do!

In any case, parents can hope that giving children this
opportunity to commune with God at home will develop a
religious background and feeling upon which to build their
more mature concepts. They should also gain a good feeling
about the unity and stability of the family which is theirs and
of the home in which they live.

For us, as parents, participation in family worship is witness to the children of our belief in God, in prayer, and our
efforts to live according to the principles of Christ. Besides,
whatever the effort, whatever the discouragement, there is
always the inspiration and joy from sharing these moments
with children. There is no greater blessing!

Someone has said that the test of worship is that it never
leaves us exactly where we were. I have never participated in
worship with our children that I did not come away from it
with a greater understanding of both God and them.

Truly, as we parents and children share in family worship,
we bring to life the words of Jesus: "For where two or three
are gathered together in my name, there am I in the midst
of them" (Matt. 18:20, KJV).

IV

As Parents– We Seek Wisdom

Wisdom is the right use of knowledge.
To know is not to be wise.

Charles Haddon Spurgeon

No More
Idle Threats

The practice of making idle threats is one of the pitfalls of parental discipline

My son, Bruce, at seven, had strict orders not to run in the living room and dining room. Yet here he was, toy airplane in hand, racing recklessly among my precious chairs and tables. From the kitchen, where I was washing dishes, I heard his shins bumping against wood and could just visualize my prize lamp teetering precariously on its table.

My heart in my throat, I called out loudly, "Stop it, Bruce!" Then I paused, holding my hands motionless above the dishwater, listening for the silence that was supposed to follow.

But it was far from silence that I heard. The noise of Bruce's running continued, now accompanied by a steady "zoom-zoom" humming as Bruce attempted to imitate an airplane with his lips.

"Did you hear me, Bruce?" I called, raising my voice higher. "I said, *stop running.*"

For a moment I thought I had succeeded as the noises faded away, until suddenly they emerged again, louder than ever. I realized then that Bruce had zigzagged into the hall closet which had muffled his tones temporarily. So at last, accepting the inevitable, I dried my hands and pursued my son into the field of action, the living room.

"Stop it, Bruce!" I now commanded. My voice followed

him around the room in no uncertain tones. "You know you're not supposed to run in here. If you don't quit this instant, I'll take the airplane away and you can't have it for a week."

That finally brought Bruce up short. He stopped his game and walked over to me slowly, a slender, sturdy figure in knit shirt and blue jeans, his stubborn cowlick bobbing down over one eye. He viewed me thoughtfully as though I might have just descended from Mars. Then he voiced his opinion dispassionately, "No, you won't."

"I won't?" I was incensed. "Why not? I said I would take away your airplane, didn't I? Don't you believe I mean it?"

He considered that at length. Finally, he nodded. "Yes, you mean it," he agreed. "But—you'll forget."

"You'll forget." His words so startled and disturbed me that for once I was speechless. And they could mean only one thing. Bruce, with his simple and direct child's thinking, knew me better than I knew myself. Apparently I must be shouting at him about a great many matters. Then after the air clears I forget my various threats. Else how would Bruce know?

I pondered over that rather deeply. Then I remembered, guiltily, earlier in the week when Bruce had borrowed my pen, even though he had strict orders never to use it. At that time I had threatened to take away something of his for a period so he'd remember about the pen the next time. But, it was I who hadn't remembered—on the punishment end! Since I hadn't carried out my threat, why should I have made it?

Now that I began analyzing disciplinary tactics, I thought of something else, too. It had to do with the whole episode of the airplane and the way I kept calling to Bruce from the other room. Of course, the reason for this was that I was engrossed in my dishwashing. I didn't want to break into it to chase Bruce down. I kept trying not to until I *had* to.

Wouldn't it have been better to dry my hands in the first place, go into the living room and say quietly (and mean it the first time): "Now stop it, Bruce. You know there's a rule against running in the main part of the house." In that case, it probably wouldn't have been necessary to make any threats, idle or otherwise. Bruce would have heard me, understood me, and stopped, all in one operation.

I could remember other instances where I'd been yelling at Bruce over my shoulder and repeating myself endlessly in the not so distant past. One day when he had gone to the sandbox stood out particularly. I had been cleaning the house, in a great rush to finish by dinnertime. But as the back door slammed after Bruce went outdoors I suddenly remembered the heavy rain of the night before. I knew the sandbox would be so muddy and wet that he could not play in it.

Rather than stop completely what I was doing, however, I threw open the dining room window and attempted to call to Bruce to tell him to play somewhere else. It was nearly the same story over again. At first he didn't hear me; when he did he couldn't understand "why" he couldn't play in the sand; by the time we got it settled, the legs of his jeans were damp already and his shoes were covered with wet sand. In addition, I was provoked that he hadn't obeyed me immediately and he was understandably grumpy about it all.

It seemed to me now, in retrospect, that I would have gained by having followed him out the door, caught his attention at once, and explained immediately why he shouldn't play in the sand.

That brings me to another point. On the matter of explaining things I'm rather good (at least I seem to think so). Maybe it's the suppressed orator in me. Anyway, I love to make speeches to my children. And no speeches are quite as high-sounding or full of fine phrases as those I use when I am reprimanding them for something.

Take, for instance, the time when Bruce was supposed to look after Sara, his little sister. They were playing out in front of our house, and since Sara was not allowed to cross the street alone, Bruce was supposed to watch her. Imagine my distress, however, when not too much later I found that ·

Bruce had deserted his post to play with some of his friends farther down the street.

This time I did indeed chase him down and present my ideas head on. "Look," I told him, "I can't have you going away. I gave you a job to do. It's your responsibility to take care of your sister. When I give you responsibility I expect you—"

Full in the throes of my own oratory, at first I didn't notice how confused Bruce looked. But presently it was borne in upon me with what bafflement his big brown eyes met mine and how, finally, his attention strayed completely. Then I stopped and thought to ask him, "Do you know what responsibility is?"

He shook his head.

"Do you know what I'm talking about?"

He still looked confused. "Well, sort of. Not exactly. I guess Sara . . ."

The fact was, of course, that he didn't understand my fine phrases. I had so cluttered the simple facts of the case with high-flown remarks that what should have been a simple matter to Bruce became an obscure one.

Another point emerged from all this. I am so anxious to leap in with my point of view that Bruce often cannot, literally, get a word in edgewise. The evening when I went to call him in for dinner and couldn't find him illustrated that perfectly. When calling his name from the front door didn't bring a response, I then phoned his friends. Since he wasn't at their homes, I searched for him among the swings and slides at the school yard.

I had given up in despair when Bruce suddenly appeared, much surprised at being wanted.

"Where were you?" I immediately leaped upon him verbally and recited my whole tale of woe about trying to find him. Then I went on to another point. In our family it is one of our main tenets that each one of us, including Mother and Dad, keeps everyone else informed as to his whereabouts.

"You know it's one of our rules that we all tell one another where we're going." I went on—and actually—on and on.

"Well, listen," explained Bruce indignantly when I'd spent myself. "I did tell you where I was going. I yelled at you when I went out. I thought I heard you answer back."

"Oh," I said lamely. "Was that what you said? I was busy in the basement and I guess I wasn't really listening."

But the trouble is that after I've delivered a lecture, it doesn't always end this well. Bruce was often too discouraged or browbeaten to offer any response at all when I finally might think to ask him, "Now, what have you to say?" That means I often didn't hear his side of the story, if there was one, and there usually was. Whereas if I started out immediately on a cheerful note of tolerance—"I've been looking all over for you. How come you didn't tell me this time where you'd be?"—I'd learn immediately what he had to say. After all, what he has to say is often as important as what I have to say, when I get right down to it.

Actually, it isn't hard to change from an over-the-shoulder, idle-threat, lecturing, one-sided parent to a better one, to the benefit of both your child and yourself.

First of all, now when I have instructions to give, I stop what I'm doing, go and deliver them face-to-face. Undivided attention never hurt any problem and usually helps to solve it faster, I find.

Second, I curb my tendency to use fine phrases and express my wishes in simple language.

Third, I try to ask my children at once their point of view on the matter in question. Getting this statement before I give mine often clears up some questions immediately without any fuss.

Finally, I try to think before I speak as to what kind of discipline is going to be meted out, if any. Many matters turn out to be merely annoying (particularly when I'm tired) and not serious enough for discipline. It's better to bite my tongue and not threaten than to threaten and not carry out the threat.

On other matters, those which turn out to be really basic,

there is only one rule, "Mean what I say the first time and stick to it." This goes for any sort of punishment or decision, and for serious or trivial misdemeanors.

Sometimes I slip, of course, and speak before I think, or make a threat too quickly. But now when I say something, I mean it, or on the rare occasions when I am just too hasty, I honestly explain and retract. But I don't make *idle* threats anymore.

This concept has helped me; it has helped my children. They know finally where they stand discipline-wise and don't have to put up with a mother who talks idly and too much.

The Importance
of Snatched Moments

**Don't wait to find time to be with
children; make time by using precious
moments snatched from the day's routine**

Before I had any children, I had a notion that there would
be a time in every day, as quiet and precious as Henry Wads-
worth Longfellow described in "The Children's Hour." But
now that I have three children, I know that, for the most
part, the Children's Hour is as dead as a dodo.

Yet I cling to the idea that time is one of the greatest gifts
we can make to our children, and that the little, shared
moments are the ones remembered. Snatched moments, I call
these, sandwiched in between other jobs.

For instance, our older daughter, along about first or second grade, never tired of playing "the three little pigs" with
me. The time she preferred was just before dinner; the place,
in the kitchen. There, while I finished my preparations for the
meal, she would hide away in her little corner between the
kitchen cupboard and the hot-air register. Then, having decided which one of us would be the wolf and which one the
pigs (we took turns), we started our story, huffing and puffing
and blowing away two pigs to the glorious moment when the
third pig, victorious over the enemy, cooked the wolf in his
pot for supper!

The unfortunate part of snatched moments for me, however, is that so often they come at times when I'm not in the
mood to play. As far as I'm concerned, the neat, tidy Chil-

dren's Hour idea is easier. But I've found that unless I snatch these moments *when* they come, they won't return.

Imagine how I groaned to myself the day my seven-year-old son, home from school with a cold, decided to put on a play in the bathroom. He was very businesslike about it and made all the preparations, chiefly stringing up a piece of old blanket for a curtain between the washbowl and the towel rack, and assembling his sister's five dolls. He was going to put on five acts, he announced, each featuring a doll singing and dancing.

Of course, the main thing he needed besides this ludicrous arena was an audience. I was it. Snatching for him a few moments from my cleaning, I left him beaming.

Actually, if snatched moments were not in the class of interruptions, and as such, sometimes annoying, they would often have a therapeutic value, such as my changing pace from the cleaning for a little while to watch my son's play.

Another time it didn't really hurt me to drop what I was doing and run out back to see the prowess my son was developing on the "monkey bars." "Come out, come out," he called, and dragging me by the hand demanded I stand there while he and his friend Joe went through their routine—clapping hands, swinging down, and then ending up hanging by their knees.

"That's great. You're surely getting good," I called as my son smiled happily. It was what he'd been hoping for. And in a few minutes I was back in the house. I had to admit it hadn't really interfered with my precious program a bit.

However, being human, there are times when I'm short of temper and strength, when I am interrupted altogether too often with snatched moments. And it is then I remember the comment of my neighbor, whose children were well along in school. She often looked across the hedge that separated her yard from ours and said feelingly: "Enjoy your little children as much as you can. They stay small such a short time."

I didn't realize what she meant then, but I do now that our own children are older. The snatched moments come less and less frequently. Instead of wanting Mother and Dad to do things with them, they turn increasingly to their friends.

Our younger daughter was just six when one Sunday she came to her daddy and me. "Come out in the yard!" she commanded, taking our hands. Once there, she seated us in the grass. "Now, wait a minute," she said.

Back into the house she went and came out with the family Bible. "Sit still," she continued. "This is church. I'm the minister."

Holding the Bible in her two hands, open as she had often seen it on the lectern in our church, she began to pray. "God bless," she said, then fumbled for words and went on with part of her bedtime prayer. Finished, we raised our heads and she said, "Now I'll talk—"

As we listened to her, we were torn between the desire to laugh and the urge to cry, from love of her. It all took only a few moments, snatched from Dad's Sunday-afternoon nap on the davenport, and Mother's dishwashing.

It was this daughter, too, who liked to help me cook. Help? I'll admit she did do a good job on greasing the cookie sheets, a task I'm not too fond of. With her whole hand flat on the tin, she made like she was finger-painting and probably would have kept it up all morning if I hadn't reminded her that there is more to baking cookies than greasing the sheets.

Later, her hot little hand joined mine on the spoon that was stirring the batter (it seemed a little awkward). The egg she tried to break skidded around (and landed in a puddle on the floor). And she fed so many nuts into the nut chopper I didn't have to chop nuts again for two months (besides, she popped a few nutmeats into her mouth every third turn of the chopper). But the beautiful thing about it was that we were together, doing something she wanted to do *with* me. Weighing this against the bother and the bit of extra time it took —which was more important?

I can think of those trips we took in the car too, the youngsters in the backseat demanding to play games as we drove along. Not content with counting red barns or white cars that we passed, they wanted to play "My father owns a grocery store and he sells P——." Persimmons, pastry, potatoes, potato chips, the items sometimes made a long list before the correct answer was arrived at, wherewith the questioner always crowed a little in triumph at how everyone had been fooled. Then the turn passed to the one who had given the correct answer. "My father owns a grocery store and he sells A——" (or G or M) and so on.

No, the children weren't content to play this game by themselves, or the several other games they thought up. Mother and usually Dad, the driver, had to play. This didn't take any time, only nervous energy if, after frantic packing to get off on the trip in the first place, I felt I'd like to be quiet, just for a minute.

Again, though, these are fun times, times that come for only a short period and then disappear.

All these experiences led me to a resolution to do my best to catch hold of snatched moments and make use of them. I've tried my best to follow through, with some relapses, I'll admit, but with more successes than failures, I hope. I believe that we can never afford to be "too busy" (or too tired or too anything else) when children bring these moments to us. The early years are the golden years for these moments. Children are full of ideas, eager, active, and still largely home-centered in their interests.

Snatched moments they are indeed, making family memories that not only we will cherish when we are older but that our children will cherish, too.

Confidences Must
Be Earned

**The parent who invites the confidences
of children knows what they are doing
and what they are likely to become**

I had my mind on a million matters that noon. The paper-hanger was coming, little Sara was home from kindergarten with a cold, the water heater wasn't working right, and I was late with lunch. When my twelve-year-old daughter Jane burst in from school I paid her small heed.

"The most exciting thing happened this morning," she cried, coming directly into the kitchen. She stood there, her eyes shining, her voice relating enthusiastically a tale of which, in my haze, I only made out snatches. "And so Jerry said it wasn't his fault and then the teacher said—" She broke off, her voice suddenly dismal. "Why, you aren't listening, Mother!"

Indeed I wasn't and I had to admit it.

"I'm sorry," I apologized lamely. "What was it you said?"

"You're just not interested," accused Jane. "It doesn't matter what I said." Her voice trailed off as she went to hang up her jacket.

"It does matter. But I've got so much on my mind, Jane," I tried to explain. Belatedly I left the luncheon sandwiches I was making and followed Jane across the room. "Tell me again, won't you?"

"No," said Jane. And coax though I would, she wouldn't repeat the story for me.

It happened to me. Has it happened to you? I just naturally (though unintentionally) muffed this moment with my daughter. And by the time I got my mind off my seemingly important adult thoughts, Jane was out of the notion of sharing her small confidence with me.

Not that that particular story about Jerry and the teacher was so important in itself—it wasn't. But I've always made one of my goals of motherhood that of seeking the confidences of my children. And I've found I have to listen to a whole lot that isn't important—and like it—to be able to share with them the small bits and pieces of their lives that are important.

But even with the best of resolutions, sometimes I find I'm off the track leading to my goal. So after this happened with Jane, I began to wonder how good a listener I really was with my children. As a result, I took my head down out of my usual adult clouds and began to watch myself.

I was dusting the living room the next day when seven-year-old Bruce came in with a tale about how his friend Johnny took his truck and how he told Johnny he wanted it back and how . . .

It was the sort of story that, if I listened to it, I would gain a good deal of insight into how my Bruce's mind worked, how he reacted to conflict, what his relationship was to his friends. But I caught myself saying "yes" and "no" vaguely in the proper places over one shoulder as I went on dusting assiduously.

That same day little Sara interrupted me when I was making my shopping list. She wanted to tell me a long tale about her imaginary playmate Denny and how he colored a picture for her and then spilled the crayons on the floor. Before I thought, I found I was merely waving my pencil at her, my mind still on the number of cans of fruit we'd need next week, and saying absently, "Uh-huh. How awful. Well, you go pick the crayons up like a good girl."

Yes, I discovered I was doing this a good deal of the time —not paying much attention to what my children were telling me, though I well know these little confidences build gradually into a revealing picture of character I couldn't secure any other way. Worse than that, perhaps, by my not being very interested I was discouraging them from confiding in me. Children talk freely when they are little. They won't do so when they are older unless I convince them along the way I'm willing and eager to listen.

Yet it isn't hard to be an interested listener. The next time Jane burst into the kitchen I dried my hands at once, left the sink, and gave wholehearted attention to the story she was telling me.

She was saying with complete unselfconsciousness, almost as she had that other day: "It's so exciting. Ruth has this chance to go to this really special radio broadcast but she's already promised to help her Girl Scout leader that day." And on and on telling what Ruth said and what Ruth's Scout leader said, ending finally with an anxious, hopeful plea, "What do you think she ought to do, Mother?"

I considered the matter carefully, not because it would make the slightest difference to Ruth, but because it was wonderful that Jane wanted my opinion. "Well, I think if it's terribly important about the broadcast, Ruth should ask the Scout leader to free her to go and to let her help some other time. But if she promised the Scout leader, and if the leader doesn't want to excuse her, why, then she has no choice but to keep her promise."

Jane considered this thoughtfully. "Yes, I guess you're right," she agreed finally. Then her mind darted on, back to her current, catchall phrase. "Isn't it exciting?"

The story was exciting about Ruth, yes, but I was more excited about my plans to be a better listener with my children. Actually, I find full interest in what they say takes little more time than half interest. Jane, Bruce, and Sara usually have just so much to relate and no more. When they have contented themselves with knowing I have heard them out, they are as eager as I am to be about other business. On the other hand, half interest leaves them baffled and undecided.

Often they hang around heckling, trying other ways to get my attention.

The other requisite is, of course, for me to be there when they want to talk. Both at lunchtime and in midafternoon after school are important. At lunch, with a little planning, I can arrange it so I can give undivided attention to their little stories.

In the afternoon I'm often at my desk. Disconcerting as it sometimes is to be interrupted, I've formed the habit of turning my back on my work when the influx from school begins. In addition, there is a comfortable old-fashioned rocker by my desk. It gives me a real thrill when Jane drops down in it for a little chat before she changes into jeans and goes off with her girl friends. Bruce usually roams about, from my room to his, dropping remarks as he goes. Sara, home from kindergarten, leans against my desk, fiddling with the pencils, while she asks me questions.

Now that Jane sometimes goes out at night, I try to make it a point to be around when she comes in. And we have a regular chat about the day's happenings when she first gets into bed.

These confidences that my children give me place an obligation on me, too. Bruce and Sara seldom know or care whether or not I repeat what they tell me. But Jane often says: "Now don't tell a soul, will you, Mother? It's a secret."

Once I did violate her confidence and I'll never do it again. I was chatting on the phone with Ruth's mother, one of my best friends. Inadvertently I repeated a bit of information Jane had told me about Ruth. "Jane said Ruth doesn't want to go to camp because she thinks—"

Even before I had finished my sentence I could hear Jane, who was in the next room, calling me. "Don't tell that, Mother, I told you not to."

Actually, I didn't think it important and I hadn't known she said not to tell. But now I'm especially careful about it. Most of what Jane tells me is "undercover stuff." I know I can never retain her confidence if I repeat all over the neighborhood what she tells me.

The hardest thing, perhaps, is to hold my tongue with Jane when she tells me something of which I don't approve. It's not always her friends who are at fault. Sometimes it's Jane herself on matters I can't ignore. But a few times I've tried jumping in with both feet and telling Jane what I thought right then and there. It never works. I may, after a time, convince Jane she's wrong, but what happens then is that she grows wary about expressing herself freely to me.

Even if I have to bite my tongue to hold it during some story Jane tells me, I do it now, making a mental note of what I don't approve. I find I can always bring it up later and get across my point without making Jane feel she made a mistake in telling me that particular story.

The gratifying thing is that all of this dovetails nicely into the job of daily living and gives zest to the pattern of it. Once I was guest at a luncheon when one of the women launched into a story about an incident in Bruce's room at school. Some of the little boys got to acting up. They threw erasers; some of them talked back to the teacher when she tried to stop them; there was general pandemonium which the principal had to settle.

I found myself listening avidly, but with equanimity. I had heard the story already from Bruce and knew his part in it. I knew what he thought about it and he knew what I thought. But the mother on my left was distressed. "My Billy didn't mention a word to me," she wailed on hearing the story. "I wonder if he was one of the bad ones. He never tells me anything. I never know what he is doing."

Well, I believe firmly that I can't be a good parent if I don't know what my children are doing. I grant that it's not always easy to find out, and some children are much more willing to talk than others. But I'll certainly never succeed unless I make an effort to listen to all they do tell me, trivial and fragmentary though it may seem at the time.

One thing I've discovered: Serious confidences cannot be

forced. There are times and moods for them and children drop them into your ears at the most unexpected moments. When one of these shining times occurs it sets my heart to singing. It makes me thankful that as the mother of Jane, Bruce, and Sara I am gaining, bit by bit, knowledge of what they are doing and becoming.

By inviting my children's confidences I hope, too, I'm becoming a trusted friend—as well as a parent—and thus from my experience will be permitted to guide them better in the way they ought to go.

Facing
the Experts

Don't hesitate to be yourself as a parent; it will pay in the end

One day I overheard my young son and daughter discussing an imminent trip to the pediatrician. "I hate those shots he gives," my son remarked ruefully. And added (not too accurately), "I wish I'd been born before needles were invented —in the olden days."

Well, sometimes in my lower moments I wish I'd been born in "the olden days," too, but for a different reason. In the days of my grandparents, I have a notion, it was simpler to be a parent. I'm pretty sure all there was to it then was that when you had a baby, without any fanfare you became a parent, *period.* No one questioned your ability to be one, and a good one, at that.

Nowadays parents have a couple of choices. One is to imitate the olden days and become parents, period, without benefit of anything other than instinct to guide them. The other choice is more complicated. Many child-guidance experts seem to reason that for practically any field you can mention nowadays there are courses to take, training sessions to attend, directives to follow. Why not for parenthood too? Certainly no field is more important. Thus, books have been published, articles written, experiments conducted with youngsters by pediatricians, educators, and those in the child-development field, the results of which purport to give parents a few foolproof methods for raising children.

Our first child was born during the height of this specialization theory. Being eager to do my best, I tried to follow all the new recommendations. I was supremely confident that I was right, and our baby was raised literally "by the book." Luckily, she turned out to be healthy and happy too.

Then, ten years later, I learned the worst. The "experts" had reversed themselves! Keeping a baby on schedule was a mistake. "Demand feeding" was better. Rocking was in, crying was out. You didn't fit the baby to the household routine; baby should come first and the household fitted to the child.

With that, many mothers, myself included, went back on the experts in disgust.

But perspective always helps, and now, two children more and some years later, I can view these same experts with a little more unprejudiced attitude. My younger daughter came to me once after a conversation with her grandfather. "What do you know!" she exclaimed, wide-eyed. "When Granddaddy was a little boy, they didn't have bubble gum." That they didn't have experts either is also true. And although the experts do not sway parents now as they did some years back, they are still around and always will be—with their experiments, their studies, and their conclusions, some of them not yet fully drawn. In that way we cannot really go back to the olden days.

Perhaps there is a middle ground for parenthood, halfway between the experts—patently sincere, but also human enough to make mistakes—and the olden days. If I could do it over (and what parent would not like a second chance!), that is the way I would take: much more belief in myself as a good parent with good common sense, following my own instincts, but still being willing to read and profit by (but not giving blind obedience to) what the experts have to say. Personally, today when I am faced with a problem, I like to "read up on it," then weigh it in the light of what "they say" *and* my own opinion, and then proceed from there.

I try not to forget, too, that no matter how much reading

and studying I do, each childhood problem, in the last analysis, becomes a very personal one, relating to one particular child. And each child is different in at least two ways: different because of heredity and environment, and different in rate of development.

Even though I have often commented on this latter fact and thought I believed it, it really didn't become completely evident to me until I taught kindergarten for a short period. I wish that every mother could have this valuable experience for a while!

Here I had about thirty children in the five- to six-year age level, all supposedly ready to go into the first grade in another few months. But no two youngsters were at the same stage of their development, though all were within the general limits of what the experts say can be expected of the "average" child at this age. Some could color well, some couldn't. Some could climb well, some couldn't. Some could print, some couldn't. But before the year was over, nearly everyone could color well, many could climb, practically all could print.

So it is with our own children. Just because my son can't ride a small two-wheeler at seven like the boy next door (who at six and a half got right on and rode away) is no sign my son won't learn to ride or be as good a rider as the other boy when he does learn. This ability to ride a bike is a part of his own rate of development and should not be compared with some other child's or with the "average" child's.

Likewise, I know that, as a child in our family, he inherited certain traits that affect his bicycling skill. His physical coordination is not just "super," as it is in a born athlete. (There are no "born athletes" in our family!) Besides, being quiet and nonathletic like his parents, he's not so much interested in bike-riding as he is in reading, collecting jars of bugs, or other more quiet pursuits.

We parents are lucky, really, that we have this background to give to our children. We remember our own parents, grandparents, and childhood vividly, and we can see these traits and characteristics popping up which represent *our* family. No expert with all his charts and averages can give a parent that. At best, the advice doled out can only be impersonal and based on the norm, whatever that is.

Once we were having a family argument with everyone putting in his two-cents' worth, when one of the children wailed, "We're not a bit like those blue-ribbon families you read about in the magazines." (You know the ones, in which everyone helps—even the two- and four-year-olds, and the house is shining from morning to night; where there is gay camaraderie, and brothers and sisters rarely if ever get mad at one another; where parents are self-contained and *always* sure of what they are doing!)

I, for one, am rather glad ours has not been such a blue-ribbon family, or even an "average" family. I much prefer our family, with all its ups and downs and differences, to every other family. That's what makes life so wonderful—to feel that there is nobody quite like your own son or daughter, or your own mother and dad. In this impersonal age when so much from outside assaults our eyes and our ears, sometimes we don't appreciate the very individuality that makes the members of our family so very special.

As a parent, why not read what there is to read about raising children, but read with discernment, and only then decide whether it has pertinence for the way your family does things? For no one but yourself can give your child the same meaning to parenthood. That's why being yourself as a parent is the first and most important part of your job.

When Can I Tell Them NO?

Holding back on outside civic jobs in order to give time to children in the early years is eminently worthwhile

The thought often comes to me that, if Whistler were planning to paint his mother today, he would scarcely find her in a chair in such repose. More than likely, whatever her age, she would be working outside the home, full or part time, or she would be at a committee meeting, or out serving a church supper, or working on a club program of some sort. It seems to me that she might not be around home long enough to pose for a picture at all!

An exaggerated notion of modern motherhood? Perhaps so. Still, most of us mothers nowadays carry several loads. For those who have to work outside for monetary reasons, it's one life. For others, who can and do stay at home while their children are young, it's another.

It's not old-fashioned in my book to want to stay at home with children when they're young. If you're one of those who doesn't have to work at an outside job for monetary reasons, read on. Civic and community activities will take over—if you don't watch out! And, as most of us have to admit, there are times when the load becomes too heavy, when even with the best of planning, things at home have to be sacrificed for those obligations assumed outside.

Which should come first? And how can we keep a balance between them?

For my own part, I don't pretend I've found *the* answers to these vital questions. But while rearing two daughters and an in-between son, I've found some answers that have helped.

There are deep roots to my answer to the first question, for I recall what my mother believed. "Home and family come first," was her credo. Not until I was in college did she undertake large-scale outside activity, such as serving as local YWCA president and as vice-president of the historical society.

But we of this generation have a harder time keeping "home and family first" than our parents did. We are laden with activities. We women are much more active and freer in every way. Finally (and this I find hardest to combat), outside activity is expected of us. When I am asked to do an outside job, I have to battle both a deep feeling that I *must* "do my part" and a tendency to feel guilty if I manage to say no for whatever reason.

Yet, to make the home-comes-first idea stick, it is essential to learn to say no, and it is necessary to formulate ideas ahead of time as to which activities are going to warrant an unwavering *no*.

The first such idea that I adopted I also borrowed from my mother. While I was growing up, she did outside only what was closely allied to my activities or to those of my father, a busy physician. Thus, I try to keep the outside jobs I do child-related, so that they bring me closer to my family rather than pull me away. For example, when I agree to be room mother for my youngest, this means I'll get to visit school more often, grow to know the teacher well, accompany the class on trips, share with my child the fun and activities.

For the same reason I have done outside jobs related to my other children: Den mother (Cub Scouts) for my son, church school teacher for my older daughter, Brownie and Scout work for both the girls, and so on.

But in another direction I've had to part company with my mother. She had only one child to my three; besides, in those days (oh, heavenly dream!) she had a maid who "lived in." Mother could do several jobs with ease if she chose. I have to limit my activities drastically, one job per child per year, taking turns. But the very limiting is good, I think. It causes me to consider ahead of time what I will do and for whom next year. And it enables me to do one job well, rather than several haphazardly.

Mostly I try, too, not to take jobs or let the jobs I have interfere with bedtimes, or with my being home after school and at mealtimes. Once I accepted a chairmanship that was supposed to entail only a few after-children's-bedtime meetings. But as it turned out there was endless telephoning to be done, to people who could not be reached except during the dinner hour! It wasn't long before my family was groaning every time I said: "You go ahead and eat dinner; I have to make some phone calls. I'll eat later."

Fortunately, my husband agrees with this home-comes-first idea 100 percent. And during the years when all the children were small, we managed pretty well to gear our social life so that it could be strongly family-centered and child-related too. Ask any parents and they'll tell you this: The early years are *the* years for family vacations at the lake, auto drives to the state park, jaunts to the zoo, spur-of-the-moment picnics. The day comes soon when the older child no longer wants to go with the family.

A family I know was eagerly planning a Florida trip during Christmas vacation. The two daughters, ages eight and eleven, were excited about it, could hardly wait. But the son, a junior in high school, had second thoughts, even third thoughts. With his own life so interesting and all-consuming at that point, go somewhere with parents and silly little sisters? He did agree to go to Florida finally after a little nudging but, sighed his mother, "This may be the last time we are able to vacation as a family."

Some families institute a regular family night, a time reserved just for doing things together. I recall reading of one man whose adult sons and their families still come home each

Sunday to celebrate family night, started years ago when the sons themselves were small.

Maybe you can do less outside the home than I can; maybe you can do more. A good way to judge how much you can do without interfering with your family life is to see how your disposition holds up. If you are often cross and upset, if either your outside jobs or your home jobs become a burden, then you'd better let up. Besides, jobs done when we are overloaded are often not done well and could beneficially be left to someone else.

Even church work should not be a drain. Some young parents solve this problem by attending the adult class which meets during the hour when their children attend church school. I solved it by teaching church school during this hour for many years and going to worship afterward.

Never forget, these activities with and for our children will be cherished memories when the years have gone by, far outshadowing remembrances of having been a good rummage-sale chairman, a superdeluxe president, or a member of any group you can name! And never forget, this time with children is *important,* even though wiping runny noses, cleaning up tracked-in mud, and joining in a monotonous game seem at the moment most *un*important.

Our little boy used to call his visits to Grandma "Grandma-time." We might call these precious years for parents "child-time." It comes only once; it lasts only a little while. Here's hoping you have enough time left over to do something outside, but when the going gets rough and there aren't enough hours to go around, doing for home and family is reason enough to turn down any outside activity in the world!

Parents Must
Try Harder

**With so many outside voices speaking
to children, parents must
try harder to impart standards and beliefs
to their children**

I can still remember running into the house one day after school, full of some tale of how Johnny had tripped me at third-grade recess and how Billy had then shoved Johnny and then . . .

My mother said, coolly interrupting me, "But where is the spool of thread I asked you to buy on your way home?"

My mouth fell open. "Oh! Oh, I forgot!"

Looking me in the eye, Mother said sternly, " 'I forgot' is no excuse."

My mother firmly believed this canon of family discipline. Why? Because her mother had impressed it on her. And what her mother, my grandmother, said was respected as law.

At times I think of those days with something resembling envy. So little of what the modern parent says is even listened to, much less regarded with respect by the modern child.

Perhaps it all started when parents became pals. Perhaps it is a result of the permissive philosophy. Certainly it has been worsened by another factor: There are so many voices talking to youngsters nowadays. No wonder parents lose out in the shuffle!

Count those voices sometime! They include radio, television, movies, comic books, magazines, newspapers, regular books among others. All of them have grown in power and influence since the turn of the century. Several of them have been in existence only a few decades.

Luckily many of the family discussions caused by these voices are more amusing than painful. I remember one such when our small son was brainwashed by radio advertising concerning a certain brand of bread. So many vitamins, so much protein, so good for your face, your figure, so good, so good . . . He nagged at me, "Why don't *you* buy This Bread?"

"Because I like That Bread better."

"But This Bread is so good for you!" He ended triumphantly, "It's *the best bread in the world.*"

I've wondered since if this was the moment when I should have sat down with my seven-year-old and explained about the New York advertising world, the soft and the hard sell, even the psychology of the "hidden persuaders." As it was, I merely lost face with him by being a stubborn mother who refused to eat "the best bread in the world" and also refused to serve it to her starving family.

On the other hand, would that the problems brought about by the multiplicity of voices were all as simple as choosing a bread to eat. The "hidden persuasions" grow and multiply as a child becomes older. In modern media, drinking is often made to seem desirable and a sophisticate's dream; unfaithfulness in marriage is portrayed with excitement and forgiveness; premarital sexual experience becomes a commonplace; having lots of money seems to be the answer to everything; shooting it out with guns is an everyday happening; and so on ad infinitum.

It's hard to know, of course, the exact amount of influence such material has. However, the fact that currently psychologists are trying to relate the high incidence of juvenile delinquency to murder and mayhem on television is just one indication of the importance of these voices which speak to children.

Actually, most conscientious parents of young children do try to screen what is seen, listened to, and read. But this is a fairly complicated process, and short of a parent serving as a policeman and looking over a child's shoulder every hour of the day, it is not as easy as it sounds. Even the most cautious parent is often brought up short by something a child has picked up, who knows where? I was considerably sobered when one of my children suggested that thunder sounded like an atomic bomb. What a frightening, if logical, comparison! My own, much more comforting (and I will admit rather archaic) childhood concept of thunder was that it was the noise God made moving furniture.

It is this very sophistication of the modern child which compounds the problem. In today's electronic world almost anything seems believable, and the more exciting it is, the more worth believing. Although most parents have the good sense and judgment not to be swayed by all the voices, children do not. And it is when parents speak out in disagreement that the trouble begins.

Should we let ourselves be beaten down, then, just because of the difficulty of being heard? *No!*

We must try harder than ever before to be sure our children know what we believe over and against the beliefs of all these others. We also must try harder than ever before to win their respect for our beliefs and standards. The time to start is when a child is young, during the important years, the early school years.

But are we what we say we are as we raise our voices to be heard? Children sense it if we are not. Do we admonish them to be fair and friendly to children of a different color but treat our own black helper with indifference? Do we scold our children for "telling tales out of school" and then indulge in petty gossip ourselves? Do we take them regularly to church school but fail to go to church ourselves?

This is not to say that all of us must be completely sterling characters, because, being human, no matter how hard we try we won't be. But children need to feel that we believe what we say and that we practice what we preach. I am reminded that this latter phrase is a cliché, but cliché or not, how can it be expressed any better?

Being what we say we are will help our voices come out loud and clear.

Next, it will help if we talk less but say more. Children sometimes become so used to droning words of command and/or opinion that they actually cease to listen: "Stop wiggling and sit still" (age three); "Don't interrupt" (age six); "Don't make so much noise" (age nine); "Get busy and practice that piano" (age twelve); "Get busy and study" (age fifteen); "Drive carefully" (age eighteen).

If we talk less but say more and *mean* what we say, we'll gain more listeners and our voices will come out loud and clear.

Finally, we should not be so afraid to be ourselves. In addition to voices that reach children nowadays, there are voices bombarding parents with instructions on how to raise children. Not only do these voices confuse us, they make us afraid of our own instincts. It's this "traumatic experience" bit which catches us. Do something wrong and it may "do" something to a child and mark him forever.

Parents haven't always felt this way.

In one area, though, we parents are pretty sure of ourselves. Where a life-and-death threat exists, such as the danger to a child who is careless crossing the street, we speak up, demand respect for safety directives, and get it. The stakes are too great to weigh what someone else might think, to listen to voices other than our own.

In many ways the stakes are just as great in these other areas of mores and manners, where outside voices are drowning out parents. Physical danger is a matter of life and death. Is not character danger a matter of life and death also?

One high school age son had a booming argument with his father about some adolescent carousing. But there was more to it than that. Finally the son said, with a sort of wonder because he thought his father Puritanical and so out of step, "I don't know how you can, but I guess you really *believe* what you've been saying." He added, under his breath, "As far back as I can remember, you've always been this way!"

Here was respect, albeit grudging, not only for a father's belief, but for a father's forthright willingness, as long as the son could remember, to take his stand.

By starting early, parents who are what they say they are, talk less, but say more, and are unafraid to make their voices loud and clear on what they believe *can* win love and respect and get their message across. But it takes work. Indeed, we parents have to try harder to win out over all those other voices competing these days for our children.

Turkeyfoot Reading Center
Confluence, PA 15424

The Masks
We Wear

**When we parents wear our masks
properly, our children can know who we are
and what we mean**

What is a mask? In our current society, it is Halloween every
day for most of us. But rather than donning an outer papier-
mâché mask which hides who we are physically, the ones I
speak of are inner-directed. They are supposed to hide who
we are—and more than that, what we are thinking and feeling.

Many masks are good and justify their use, or so we think.
Sometimes we don a mask for kindness' sake (pretending to
an ill person that he looks well when he actually looks terri-
ble), or for purposes of family peace (saying we like a wife's
new dress when actually we do not), or for purposes of en-
couragement (telling a child he has drawn a good picture of
a horse when it doesn't even resemble one).

But children start out in life completely honest and also
brutally frank. What does our wearing of masks do to them?

In the case of the good masks, we can feel that they help.
Take Sharon, young daughter of a friend of mine. Instructed
by her mother in correct table manners, Sharon was aston-
ished when a teen-age friend of her brother's came to dinner.

"You're chewing with your mouth open," she shot at him.
"Don't you know better?" "You're not using the right fork
for your salad." "Look, you haven't even opened your nap-
kin."

Later Sharon and her mother had a talk. "First I praised her for her honest approach," said her mother. "But then I pointed out that Bill was a guest in our home and as such we should be considerate of him and polite. Also, that it probably was not his fault that he did not have good manners, since very likely he had never been taught. If someone did tell him, it should be done with tact and finesse, not just blurted out as Sharon had done."

Quite an order for a girl of seven to assimilate? Indeed, yes. But these are the ways children learn to be considerate of others in our world.

Likewise, there are special masks we wear with our children that we feel are justifiable in order to help them. There is the Mask of Courage, when really we are afraid. Many a mother, terrified of storms, has hidden her feelings in order not to pass on her fears to her child.

But what about masks which are not as laudable? I recall reading about young Prince Charles of England, his loneliness because of his position and subsequent difficulty in making friends. True, he is always surrounded by people, but he said that he learned how to sense who wanted something and who offered genuine friendship.

How often we ourselves wear the Mask of Friendliness, not because we care about a person but because of who he is.

"Do you really like Daddy's boss?" Judy questioned her mother in a puzzled tone.

"Why do you ask?" returned her mother.

"Well, at home you and Daddy talk about him pretty awful, but today at his office you sounded all friendly like."

Once again, a child had seen through parent pretenses.

This is why so often it does not work when parents postpone divorce "for the sake of the children." It is hard to wear the Mask of Love when the sentiment does not come from the heart.

In fact, since the purpose of "mask" is to hide, it follows that much of what we hide is what we are ashamed of. It cannot help making our children uneasy about us.

Phyllis was playing in a corner of the room while her mother was coffee-klatching with friends. The adult talk covered several juicy stories about neighbors, particularly the separation of one couple who had a young son, Joey. Suddenly the women realized Phyllis was hanging on their every word. As they became silent Phyllis spoke up. "Why are you sorry for Joey? Is Joey sick?"

As her mother caught her breath, one woman mumbled something, ending with, "So you see, dear, we are just concerned." Yet, her effort to put on the Mask of Concern did not hide the fact that they were gossiping.

Then there was Stephen, standing with his father in the back of the church at the end of the service. His father had just remarked to a friend, "You look great this morning, but you'll look even better when I tell you this story." He had just started to whisper the bawdy tale when the minister strolled up.

Stephen could scarcely believe his eyes. In a wink his father became another man. He smiled benignly at the minister, remarked that the sermon had been good, and how was the minister's family, anyway?

Who, or what was his dad, really? The bawdy joker wearing the Mask of Hail-Fellow-Well-Met with friends? Or the pious citizen under his Mask of Holiness at church? Besides, Stephen had noticed that his dad boasted at home a lot about how important he was at work where he made people jump when he gave orders. Was this his true dad, or was he putting on a Mask of Importance for his family? Stephen had seen that very often he wore the Mask of Meekness when his mother set her foot down.

Is it any wonder Stephen was bewildered? So often when we adopt a different mask in each new situation, the self and its identity get lost. As a result, in our use of masks we fool neither others nor ourselves. Apparently one of the greatest problems of people today is the fear of taking an honest look at themselves.

These, then, are the masks we should watch out for—the

ones which hide our real selves. With a little effort we can develop more awareness and through this begin to deal with masks, our own and those of others, more constructively.

To get a further view of this we decided to hold a discussion in our own family. We were amazed at how instinctively perceptive our children were of the whole subject of masks, without reading or indoctrination from anyone. As an example, they brought up a family we know that wears the outer Mask of Perfect Love for their children, but beats them unmercifully in private. What seems to offend our youngsters most is the mask that covers phoniness.

Sara also mentioned a friend "who is nice to everyone to their faces and then cuts them down to their backs." On the other hand, the kids were more sympathetic with a boy who boasts that everything he has is bigger and better than anything of theirs. Though they did not exactly understand why, they sensed that he has to find some means to feel superior. So they shrugged him off without resentment, saying merely, "He can't help it."

We talked then, briefly, about how masks can be protective in this way. They laughed when I told about Sara, as a small child, always replying, "Yam, yam," meaning, "I am, I am." This was her mask saying "Yes, I'm doing what you ask," when she had not tried to do what we asked at all. They agreed that when we grow older we should not have to hide behind a mask this way. We should be willing to take responsibility, honestly, for what we do or do not do, or for that matter, for who we are.

This brought us to the word "honesty" as the key to avoid a bad use of masks, or perhaps the word "genuine," as Prince Charles used it.

But how do we know when to be honest, realizing that absolute honesty is sometimes cruel?

We can find help on this in the Bible. In his letters to the Ephesians (4:15), Paul suggests an answer in his phrase, "speaking the truth in love." To put it in other words, while we cannot throw away our masks entirely, those which meet the test of love can never hurt others or ourselves.

More important, when we speak our children can then know exactly who we are and what we mean. It follows that they will not feel so great a need for masks themselves as they grow and become parents in their turn.